Endorsements

"I couldn't put this book down. As one who has been betrayed, I longed to understand: How could someone who claimed to love me fail to see and hear my pain? How could they lose all feeling for me? How could I have prevented this from happening? Am I to blame? Through his own excruciating journey as the betrayer, Jeremy courageously explains what I wanted to know: exactly how sin hardened his heart, diminishing everyone he cared about and deafening him to their cries. Until Jeremy turned back to the Lord, he was blind to the ones he had loved the most. This is an important book about the deadly grip of sin, the gift and process of repentance, and the overwhelming, unending love of God."

—Vaneetha Rendall Risner
Author, *Walking Through Fire* (Thomas Nelson)

"*The Bellowing of Cain* is a compelling story of someone who, through his sin, damaged his own life and the lives of others. That story, in itself, isn't unusual. What's unique is Jeremy Grinnell's willingness to tell with unflinching candor his story of failure and shame so that others might benefit from his hard-won wisdom and enter more deeply into the reality of God's extravagant grace. This is a must-read book which will stretch and enlarge our imagination for what restoration and redemption can look like in the body of Christ."

—Sharon Garlough Brown
Author, *Sensible Shoes* (IVP) and *Shades of Light* (IVP)

"This book hurts—it hurts to read, it hurts to reflect, it even hurts to ponder the way forward. But it hurts in the service of helping, for if there is no help for Cain, there is no help and no hope for any of us. Let the redemptive healing begin."

—**Wendy Widder**
Professor of Old Testament, Bethel College,
Author of *Daniel* (Story of God Commentary)

"*The Bellowing of Cain* offers wisdom from a voice we don't often hear from in the aftermath of a scandal caused by a destructive sin. Not the voice of one wounded by what's been done, but the voice of one who did it—one who has plumbed the depths of repentance and grace and found that God is both able and willing to redeem all things. I want all my friends in ministry to read this book! May it stir our imaginations for what a full expression of grace and redemption could look like in the Church!"

—**Brian Blum**
Lead Pastor, Frontline Community Church
& the Zero Collective Network

"This is the book I've been looking for and couldn't find. It's an unflinchingly honest account about the messy complexities of sin and grace, repentance and forgiveness. It invites us to a gospel hope in the slow work of God."

—**Shalini Bennett**
Professor of Spiritual Formation, Grand Rapids
Theological Seminary

THE
BELLOWING
of
CAIN

HOPE for Those Who've Blown It

JEREMY GORDON GRINNELL

ST.ASINUS
PUBLISHING

St. Asinus Publishing is an affiliate of Gordon Greenhill Book and Audio,
Grand Rapids, Michigan

Requests for permission to quote from this book should be directed to:
Permissions Department, St. Asinus Publishing, 7020 Fox Meadow NE, Rockford, MI
49341, or contact us by e-mail at bellowingofcain@gmail.com.

Names of some individuals have been changed in order to preserve their anonymity.

Edited by David Lambert
Copy Edit by Jean Kavich Bloom
Interior design by Beth Shagene
Cover Design by Jam Graphic Design

ISBN: 978-0-9996795-6-2 (softcover)
ISBN: 978-0-9996795-7-9 (ebook)

Printed in the United States of America

First printing, 2022

CONTENTS

PART 3.
FINDING NEWNESS:
Perspectives for Starting Over and Finding Hope

PREFACE

WHEN I TURNED FORTY, I WENT INSANE FOR A LITTLE while. When I came back, I found myself all alone. That isolation drove me crazy. I was surprised to find that this second madness—the madness of solitude—left me more changed than the first one. Says Linda Loman in Arthur Miller's play *Death of a Salesman*, "Life is a casting off." Resignation fills her voice because everything she really loves is being slowly stripped away by her husband's self-deception and pride. But out of her pain, she speaks deep wisdom.

And Jesus agrees with her.

He told us gaining heaven might involve even the loss of an eye or a limb. Now, if American Airlines limits me to a couple of carry-ons, you can bet the baggage policy for the celestial journey will be even more restrictive. Whatever our possessions in the New Kingdom, they'll be made up primarily not of things we've brought with us but with things we're given when we arrive.

This doesn't mean the stuff we have here and now doesn't matter. Rather, it means this ever-diminishing quality is a feature of everything we have. We can't keep the stuff, whatever we do. The wisest people keep this quality in mind as they contemplate their possessions, dreams, labors, and legacy. Not only does life end with but every moment consists of an inevitable casting away of things we'd hoped we'd get to hang on to.

That is the spirit with which I write this book.

I don't want to write it, but I'm told I have to.

I'm told the church needs to hear stories like mine. I'm told it will help other people who travel similar roads. I'm sure that's all true. Even so, I don't want to write it. It feels like a casting away of things I want to hang on to. It feels like death to me.

There's no alternative, though. Sometimes you have to die a little bit in order to live a lot more. It's a farming premise—first the seed must perish. And since the only things that qualify for resurrection are dead things, let's get busy dying. There are many books I want to write, but they all seem to run through the grave door of this one. So today I write the book I'm ashamed of so that one day I may write books of which I can be proud. I hope you won't think less of me for such a self-serving motive. There are better reasons to think less of me. Choose one of those.

So if I have to write this book, I won't waste your time pandering. I'm not writing a Christian self-help book. We have those in abundance, and although valuable, they sometimes leap over a basic principle. They often introduce their "Christian response" to adversity too soon—as if sufferings are valuable only once they're baptized.

But that's not our actual experience with suffering. We don't meet it first as saints but rather as mere animals. Suffering plays on our senses first as simple pain or sorrow. Eventually, we might process it more rationally—as outraged humans. Only later— sometimes—can we learn to accept it with grace as Christians.

The raw animality and the unredeemed rage often receive short shrift from churchly writers because these earlier stages are perceived as unworthy or unspiritual. But many great truths are learned—can *only* be learned—by taking these earlier moments seriously, precisely as we feel them. Much is lost when we prematurely rush faith to the front lines in order to temper and temporize our pain. Show me the God-fearing man who says bravely of his suffering, "It hurts but little for I have Christ," and I will show you another equally God-fearing man, sitting on an ash heap, scraping his sores with broken pottery, lamenting he was ever born. Which feels more honest to your own experience of suffering?

Understand, then, that this is to be a medium-rare account of a man who built a wonderful life and career, of the depression and life-destroying choices that followed, of the sorrows these brought to him and everyone he ever knew, and yes, of the manner in which his faith preserved him. But we'll not get to that last space on the board except by means of the squares that precede it.

There's the point. We mustn't pretend every space on the board of life looks alike. Not all reflect the saint. Some are merely animal groanings, and no amount of baptismal ablution can make them otherwise, nor need it. God is content to use the animal as well as the saintly—perhaps even prefers it. This is how you discover the deep truth that things you thought true on one square can become false on another.

This shouldn't surprise us. At our moment of, say, greatest bitterness, bitterness may be the most legitimate response even if some future point reveals that bitterness is one of those heavy bags that must be set down and left behind. For me, both things were true in their turn, and I have not sought here to make one true at the expense of the other. It's another case of *casting off*. I have been bitter; then I have been content. The second gained only by the passing away of the first—perhaps only by passing *through* it.

Which square was the right one? That's the wrong question. The real question is something like, "Where are you in the journey? How many steps have you taken? Oh, that many? Well, then, of course you're bitter. You're standing on the bitterness square. Only wait a bit ..."

That doesn't make bitterness an end—God forbid—but only a single and perhaps inevitable footfall on the way. You can neither jump over that spot safely nor remain ditheringly in it. You must walk bracingly through that square at whatever speed you can and then leave it. That is what growth looks like. We are temporal creatures. We cannot occupy all the squares in the game at the same moment. We leave behind one square so we can occupy one further along. Whether that square contains a snake or a ladder is often irrelevant; it's just the next square.

When we do happen upon the snake, a little resilient stoicism may be more helpful than a host of biblical maxims. So be it. Faith is a longer-term game—revealed in the will to keep walking and in the belief that the game ends on a ladder rather than on a snake. The most vital tenet of our faith is that life continues even after life itself has been cast off.

—Jeremy Gordon Grinnell

CAIN SPEAKS

Once upon a time there were two brothers. The older's name was Cain, and the younger was called Abel. Now, in the course of his life, Cain experienced a great disappointment with his God, and in the midst of the agony of his soul, he decided somehow his brother was the cause—or at least a constant reminder of it. So it came to pass ...

Cain said to his brother Abel, "Let us go out to the field." And when they were in the field, Cain rose up against his brother Abel and killed him.

Then Yahweh his God said to Cain, "Where is your brother Abel?"

He said, "I don't know; am I my brother's keeper?"

And Yahweh said, "What have you done? Listen; your brother's blood is crying out to me from the ground! And now you are cursed from the ground, which has opened its mouth to receive your brother's blood from your hand. When you till the ground, it will no longer yield to you its strength; you will be a fugitive and a wanderer on the earth."

Cain bellowed, "My punishment is greater than I can bear! Today you have driven me away from the soil, and I shall be hidden from your face; I shall be a fugitive and a wanderer on the earth, and anyone who meets me may kill me."

Then Yahweh said to him, "Not so! Whoever kills Cain will suffer a sevenfold vengeance." And Yahweh put a mark on

*Cain, so that no one who came upon him would kill him. Then
Cain went away from the presence of Yahweh and settled in
the land of Nod, east of Eden.*

—Genesis 4:8–16, adapted from the NRSV

I USED TO TEACH SYSTEMATIC THEOLOGY TO SEMINARY STU-
dents. It doesn't matter what systematic theology is—at least
it seldom mattered to my students. They only wanted to know
whether I could answer their questions about Christianity and
the Bible. If I could explain hard things in simple terms. They
wanted to know not if something was *true* (although that occasionally mattered) but whether it was *useful.* While this is bound
to annoy a professional theologian, in fairness to them, it is possible for a thing to be both true and irrelevant.

I spent a lot of class time working with the stories in early
Genesis—the creation of the world and humanity, the fall into
sin—for exactly these reasons. While students sometimes struggled with how these stories could be *true,* they seldom questioned
that they were *useful.* They are the Christian explanation for most
of our human experience.

First, they reveal why so many things in life are good and
beautiful. A good God made all these good things so humans
might use and enjoy them in ways that display God's glory in the
world. Second, these stories explain why the world *we* inhabit
is so filled with wretchedness and sorrow. Humanity rebelled
against this good God, shattering both themselves and all that
had been entrusted to their care—which was everything. Further,
these stories even speak of redemption. God declares that broken things can be restored—promises, in fact, that they *will* be
restored, not by mere human efforts but by that same good God
stooping down to work through human hands. This is the first
hint of a redeeming Messiah.

I rehearse all of this because this book is specifically about the difficulty we have moving from the second to the third movements of the story—from Fall to Redemption.

My students were usually more interested in the transition from the first to the second movement—Creation to Fall. They would ask how Adam and Eve's eating an apple—admittedly a small thing—could cause the whole world to go to heck in a handbasket. The punishment seems so much greater than the crime. Our hearts stiffen under the idea that small mistakes can bring such great destruction. It doesn't seem just. I understand the question, and while I believe good answers exist, I admit that on the surface, it chafes.

But our expectations about justice are fickle. Not once in my fifteen years of teaching graduate theology and many years of pastoral ministry did anyone ever ask the same question of Cain's fall from grace. I have heard Cain called a whiner. I've heard him labeled impenitent. I've even heard him called fortunate because his punishment should have been harsher. In his first epistle, St. John even makes Cain, rather than his father, the ultimate foil to Christ.[1] Following John's example, early church writers use Cain as the archetype of the Fall at least as often as they so speak of Adam. He is even considered by some the father of an entire line of evil descendants, standing against the righteous line of his brother Seth. In this view, the children of righteousness are always persecuted by the children of evil—in other words, the unredeemable children of Cain.

I do not dispute the truth or usefulness of any of this. I don't wish to downplay the evil Cain did in any way. I don't question whether his punishment was just. But I am intrigued by our lack of curiosity about what became of him, of his emotional and spiritual journey after his banishment.

He goes "away from the presence of Yahweh" and is an outcast. That is the end of our knowledge of and interest in him. We don't care if his heart ever changed. He is just an outcast.

We're not curious about any lessons his banishment may have taught him. He is just an outcast. We're not concerned about the nights of solitude, shame, and sorrow that were his. We don't care, because he's just an outcast. He may bellow his grief and misery at a cold and indifferent sky, but no one is there to hear. He is the archetypal perpetrator of evil and as such lies beyond redemption.

Yet Cain's journey matters desperately to me, for I am like Cain. I, too, have cause to wonder whether I really can move from Fall to Redemption. For all our pious rhetoric, I wonder, is redemption really available for people like Cain—people whose wounds are entirely self-inflicted?

I also bellow and get no reply.

A Son of Cain

I no longer teach at a seminary. I no longer pastor a church. I'd like to say the details don't matter, but they do. If all you knew about Cain was his exile, you would wonder, *Exiled for what?* And you'd be right to wonder. Cain's crime was not a small thing. It does matter. So I will lay out my failures here at the beginning (with more detail to come) so that you can understand why Cain now matters to me.

In 2013, I was justly convicted of *surveilling an unclothed person.*

That's right. I'm a peeping tom.

If it reddens your cheeks a little bit to contemplate a seminary professor and respected pastor doing such a thing, I'll understand. I'm still surprised by it myself. It's not the sort of thing a younger me would have expected to be part of my biography.

Sadly, however, it is not the worst thing I did. Oh, in a legal sense, it was, insofar as I broke no additional laws. But in a moral sense, the ten months preceding that choice were far worse. That was the season of the premeditated emotional affair, wherein I betrayed my wife, my children, my students, and my congregation. I lived a tortured double life—a life I both hated and freely chose. The first part of this book is the story of how I ended up there—how I became like Cain and "murdered" the closest relationships in my life.

Naturally, there is more to the story. There is always is. But I don't want any of the subsequent *context*—a word often used to deflect one's guilt—to imply that I was not responsible for my actions. This is a record of *my* choices and *my* failures. The context is only important for understanding how we get ourselves into the position where such self-destructive choices seem viable. The context is the warning. It's the school room in which, if we pay attention, we can learn the lessons that will prevent such failures in both ourselves and others.

Regarding this larger context, I think I made my best attempt at articulating it several years ago. A major Christian publisher had expressed interest in publishing my dissertation. That was gratifying. But I also knew it was no good trying to go forward without their knowing my backstory. I crafted a delicate email knowing that hitting Send would cause them to retract the offer. Nevertheless, I wrote …

> *That you are prepping a contract for my dissertation is a significant step forward for me. I have told you I left the academic world under a cloud, and so long as I was only doing* [uncredited voiceover work for your publishing house], *the details of my story didn't seem relevant.*
>
> *But we're entering a new phase wherein our reputations will depend on each other for success, and after much prayer and conversation with my wife Denise, I think it is important to give you more details lest you ever think I've not been forthcoming with you.*
>
> *In 2013, I endured a ten-month clinical depression in relation to a woman Denise and I were attempting to help*

through a home foreclosure and legal battle. I lost track of personal boundaries and became fixated on her and her family's needs. She further encouraged this obsession. It nearly destroyed my marriage and my health.

Ultimately the depression and obsession led to an indiscriminate invasion of privacy (a David-like case of being in the wrong place at the wrong time and not walking away when I should have). It was not done by design, and I attempted to resolve it with both a confession and a placing myself under the discipline of the elders, and even offered my resignation of my pastoral responsibilities at the church. Exercising her legal rights, however, she decided to press charges. The press got hold of the story, and I was publicly shamed. After which I also resigned my professorship from the university. Ultimately, rather than prolong the agony for my family, I took a plea deal, and the judge, apparently realizing the convoluted nature of the case, gave me only probation. But the public record remains ... and is ugly.

The depression mercifully broke, and my marriage was restored, but it was the beginning of two very dark years of almost total isolation. To go from a career in ascendance to unusable and unwanted was almost more than I could bear ... But God is good ...

This is what I wrote then and have included here as written except for the name of the publisher and certain personal details about the woman, who for the sake of her privacy, I will hereafter refer to as "Lorelai" after a television character to whom she bore a vague emotional resemblance. Even as I reread this account, I don't think I could improve on it for brevity or emotional distance. Of course, such a story would sound very different coming from Lorelai, or from the elders of my church, or from the dean at the seminary, or from Denise—especially Denise. I admit this. But all stories must begin somewhere. The rest will come as needed.

Why This Book?

So now I'm a child of Cain. I don't mean I've ceased to be a Christian, nor that God's love for me has slackened, nor that I feel I am beyond forgiveness. I mean that like Cain, I, too, was thrust beyond the sphere of human society because of my sin. I have bellowed at the consequences of my choices—both those that were organic and expected and those that seemed beyond the realm of the bearable. And so I ask again, when we speak of the third chapter of the biblical story—the redemptive chapter—does it exist for people like me? Am I alone in such questions?

I don't think I am.

One of the most shocking things about my journey is that in the first three years following the implosion, I had more people tell me about their own comparable journeys than in the fifteen years preceding it. I can explain this only by means of a gently cynical observation that once you're damaged goods, other people feel you're a safe person with whom to share their own failures. After all, who am I to judge?

I've had people confess to me they've done exactly what I was convicted of, only they'd never been caught. I've had pastors, missionaries, and schoolteachers confess their own emotional (and occasionally physical) indiscretions and their overwhelming ulcer-inducing fear, knowing if anyone ever knew they would be out of their positions and unemployable forever. I've listened to wives and husbands going through the same feverish obsessions over everything from losing their youth, to losing their respectability, to losing their legal freedom. I've seen their fear. The fear of being

> I write to those who live in terror of someone asking, Where's Abel? because they know that each repetition of the lie upon which their survival depends only deepens their guilt and shame.

found out, of forfeiting everything. They live in terror of someone asking, *Where's Abel?* because they know each repetition of the lie upon which their survival depends only deepens their guilt and shame.

I've seen the hunted, lost look in their eyes because they know that when it all comes out, it won't matter what demons they've struggled with. It won't matter how long they've fought to keep those demons under control. It won't matter that they did everything in their power to do the right thing even as they were also doing the wrong thing. It will make no difference at all. In the eyes of everyone, they will be the perp, and all sympathies will be with the victim. They will be cast aside.

They are not wrong to fear this.

This is what will happen.

They will be like Cain.

If you have such skeletons hiding, or if they've been dragged out and put on display on your front lawn, you know the terrors of which I speak. This book was written for you—the perpetrator, the shamed, the fugitive, the outcast. I wrote it so you may know that you are not alone. There is hope. Others have walked this road ... and have survived.

Why Focus on Perpetrators Rather Than Victims?

Now, if you're a child of Cain like me, you're probably suspicious. Who has sympathy for culprits and malefactors? Most books on surviving trauma deal with the *victim*. They ask how to survive the troubles that come from without—the diagnosis you received, the abuse you endured, the layoff you didn't deserve. Such books want to help a person grow through injuries that are not their fault.

But that's not you. That's not me. Our wounds are self-inflicted. We're the ones people blame for their pain. We're the ones people shun because we *are* at fault. Abel is dead, and we're the ones with blood on our hands. Why worry about us when there are victims to be comforted?

The question is fair and right.

This is one of the hard truths we have to accept as a starting point. Our choices have forfeited people's sympathies. They are correct to sympathize with victims. Their attention is on Abel.

And it should be.

Cain's losses are what he deserves, and it is just. I cannot disagree. Cain is guilty.

Yet even after I've agreed with God that Cain's punishment was just, a leftover remains. Even after I've remembered that Abel lost far more than Cain. Even after all the pain Cain caused his parents, his brother, the human race, and his God is accounted, a drunken sentiment still staggers around my heart crying, *But poor Cain.*

And now that I know Cain's feeling from the inside ...

Now that I know his need to bellow at the weight of his punishment ...

Now that I know the hideous shame standing behind that cry and all it tries to hide, I cannot turn my back to it. Nor can anyone who has ever made a horrible choice and lost precious things.

We must write books such as this. We must write to perpetrators as well as to victims. Not the same books, perhaps, but Christ's death was not only for victims. The cross was a criminal's death, meant to atone for criminals' deeds. A gospel of reconciliation demands a place on the shelf for this book next to all those that offer help to victims.

No book—certainly not this one—can release Cain from what he did. He did it. He must own it. Rather, the goal of a book like this is to put words to Cain's cry—and to yours—so you will know you are not the first to bray uselessly at the universe and, in that knowledge, find hope.

Final Comments Before Beginning

The following chapters form a kind of chronological development in three parts or movements. Part 1 offers reflections on the various defenses breached in the run-up to self-destruction. Part 2 discusses what it's like to watch your world crumble around you and how to face the immediate consequences—the short game. And the final section, Part 3, offers hopeful thoughts on rebuilding a meaningful life after all the immediate furor has died down—the longer journey.

As this implies, I'm addressing two types of people. First and primarily, the person who, like me, once worked in a "Christian organization"—the former pastor, church staffer, missionary, teacher, university employee—and is reeling from self-inflicted damage that has cost them their career. As you read the first section, you may well ask, *Why is he rehearsing the run-up to destruction? It's too late for me. That's not what I need.* I'm sorry to disagree, but that's actually the first thing you need. It's not about just standing back up where you are. You also need to think about how you ended up on the ground. The first section of this book is just as important to you as the others, because you blew up your life *for a reason.* Something caused it. If you don't figure that out, you're in for an encore performance.

The second reader I'm speaking to is the ministerial student, the commissioned missionary, the serving pastor, or church/parachurch staff member. For you, this book is a crash course in prevention—particularly the first section. I want you to know the warning signs, both in you and in others. I want you to avoid Cain's fate. The later sections on rebuilding should have pastoral value as you work with Cain's children in your communities.

But there is a third possible reader—the victim. Are you one of those hurt by Cain—the spouse, the friend, the congregant? In no way do I intend to marginalize your suffering. It is real, and I would not detract from it in the least. Your wounds are of central importance, but I hope you can acknowledge even through your pain that yours are not the only wounds that need the gospel. Though our wounds are different, Christ's healing work was for all of us—victims and perpetrators alike. So please understand that this book was not written primarily to you and parts of it will be painful to read. But if you've still determined to read it, my prayer is that it will give you a glimpse into the soul of the one who hurt you. That can sometimes facilitate healing.

To restate the central question, then, What's Cain to do? Can he find his way back into the human fold, or does he bellow in vain? Tragic literary figures may deserve what they get, but they are still tragic. Is redemption a mere idea or a real possibility? Is there hope for Cain?

If in the end redemption does not exist for the worst of sinners, it exists for no one.

PART 1

THROWING IT ALL AWAY

Perspectives on Self-Destruction

"I don't know what it is," answered Fiver wretchedly.
"There isn't any danger here, at this moment.
But it's coming—it's coming. Oh, Hazel, look!
The field! It's covered with blood!"

—Richard Adams, *Watership Down*

CHAPTER 1

SELF-DECEPTION

A traveler happened upon a remote village in the mountains. The people were friendly and bade him come to a great feast of welcome. Upon arriving at the table, he was revolted to find all the meat rancid and all the vegetables rotten. Unfazed by the fetid food, the villagers consumed the meal with gusto.

Staring sullenly at his plate, the traveler mumbled, "Ugh, how can they possibly eat this?"

"Just keep chewing," replied the man next to him. "Keep telling yourself you like it. You'll eventually convince yourself."

To THIS DAY WHEN I'M OUT IN PUBLIC AND HEAR SOMEONE'S iPhone give off that YOO-HOO! incoming-text whistle, I get PTSD-like tremors. I've dropped glasses of water in restaurants, frozen immovable in grocery store aisles, lost my power of speech mid-conversation. That sound was my summons. I could be called out of bed at 2:00 a.m. by that sound.

And I came willingly.

I'd never texted before. My contacts app had no names in it. This was all new to me. I didn't even own a cell phone, only my iPad. But I was being shepherded into this technology by an expert with hundreds of contacts, a master of multiple concurrent text-versations, an emoji shaman.

But as the whistles grew more frequent, I knew their meaning was changing. My wife, Denise, knew it too. At first the texts were always work related, but as things devolved, I was summoned to offer comfort, perspective, advice, or even just company.

It began in December with, YOO-HOO! *You said you thought there might be some help for my house.* And so began an eleven-month campaign of pursuing housing advocacy agencies and raising local funding to keep the mortgage from defaulting.

In February, the text read, YOO-HOO! *I can't come to work today because I can't afford daycare.* So began a nine-month stint of Denise watching the tyke along with our own newborn during work hours.

In April, YOO-HOO! *I have some legal trouble with the welfare office. Can you help?* This was the start of a seven-month effort of hunting up pro bono legal representation, contacting state representatives, and learning about policing overreach.

Then on a May evening, YOO-HOO! *I'm so lonely. I wish you were here tonight.*

And by then, I wished I were too.

Where's the Line?

While reading the preceding section, at what point did you think, *Whoa! Stop. Red flag.* You probably saw it pretty quickly. Well, I didn't. It never occurred to me that this situation was bigger than I could handle. But it should have. It was obvious. Not a single one of Lorelai's needs was I competent to deal with. I have no social work training. No law degree. I never held a public office. Never even had so much as an introductory counseling course. It wasn't even in my job description—I was a teaching pastor. I was supposed to be writing sermons.

What I was blind to, others saw clearly. My wife saw it. Colleagues in the office saw it. What kept me from seeing it? What keeps any of us from seeing our own impending trouble?

Proximity.

I was too close.

Because I knew all the complex motives behind my actions, it was actually harder for me to see which ones were really driving me. My spouse, friends, and colleagues couldn't see all those internal motivations; they saw only the actions themselves. While it's counterintuitive, when you have fewer facts, you can often make a better guess—one that's closer to the truth. Stated differently, others will jump immediately to the most probable and obvious motive for the action ... and they are often right.

They were right in my case—I was in over my head.

But I believed my own rhetoric. I wanted to help. I was a pastor. It was my job to help. That publicly stated motive was true, but it wasn't the whole truth. I was getting other things out of this as well. People who need you are pleasant to be around. They stroke the ego. They let you be their savior with all the accompanying good-feels. Further, if that person is attractive or vivacious or even just close, if they thank you profusely for caring when no one else does, how can you be sure which of your motives drives you at any given moment?

We have the ability to profess health and strength where corruption has already eaten the bone hollow. Not only profess, but believe.

We have the power to deceive not just others but ourselves.

The Truthful Lie

Self-deception is the capacity to say something false while believing it true, and few limits exist on how thorough self-deception can be. At the lowest point of that relationship—and you'll need the following chapters on depression and obsession to really understand my record-breaking limbo skills—I had convinced myself that not only did I not love my wife of eighteen years but I had *never* loved her, that our whole marriage had been a fraud—especially compared to the golden warmth I was feeling in Lorelai's presence.

This was of course demonstrably false. We'd had a remarkable and beautiful marriage. Every person who'd ever known us could have told us that, and plenty did. It's clear in the VHS tape of our wedding. The young man on stage is obviously smitten—madly in love with that lady in white.

Yet I couldn't acknowledge that truer history—not to her, not to myself. All my affections were against me. All the sentries of my soul were on guard lest I let slip the truth to myself and make plain the death into which I was willingly walking. The river of my feelings was damned at the source, and consequently, so was I—damned, that is.

But self-deceivers must be careful. They'll out themselves in the most ironic ways. Even something like alcohol, with its reputation for enabling folly, can work against self-delusion.

I could count on a cartoon hand the times I've been drunk in my life. I'm a control freak, and the feeling of not being in control is unsettling to me. That said, the drunkest I've ever been came on a night when my brother had just reamed me out over the phone for being an ass who was throwing his life away over a "woman of questionable morals." I hung up in a state of inner torment, ran out of the house, drove to the local grocer, and bought a bottle of Malbec with the words *Stark Raving* on the label. I then drove home, climbed up on the roof of my minivan in my driveway, and drank the whole bottle in twenty minutes.

That quantity of alcohol plus the speed with which I put it down left me stewed like a tomato but also gratefully numb. I eventually stumbled into the house and fell down in the dining room, unable to walk. Denise helped me up, took me to the bathroom, stripped me, and shoved me into the shower.

So slavering drunk was I that I'd lost the capacity to lie. As I fell into the shower, I remember stammering out a rambling apology, telling Denise I loved her so much, I always had, and I was sorry I wouldn't be able to tell her again in the morning. And with that she went to bed, and I sat in the shower till I was sober enough to resume my lie.

Denise and I have never spoken of that incident, but to this day I wonder if that's why she stayed—because she knew the truth. It had come out when I'd been too drunk to maintain the lie I defended when sober.

So with the truth well damned up in my soul, I stood ready to walk out of my marriage at the first sign of openness from Lorelai. I was convinced with my whole heart that the wonderful, beautiful life Denise and I had built together with our four children was all a waste and a lie.

But it was a lie that required a lot of effort to maintain.

The Hard Work of Self-Deception

That in a nutshell is the problem with self-deception. We have to work really hard at staying self-deceived. When the church counselor showed up in my office midsummer and asked if something was going on between Lorelai and me, I told her we were just good friends—and I meant it with all my heart. I believed it.

I really wanted to believe it.

I *mostly* believed it.

But I had to work at it. As Al Gore argued once upon a time, truths are inconvenient things that can be pushed aside with only varying degrees of success. Losing a fifth of your body weight in four months is a difficult thing to ignore ... but I worked diligently at it! I eventually persuaded myself that, despite my suits hanging off my frame like the scarecrow's rags, I was back to my college weight. That's a good thing, right?

I spent more time texting Lorelai on my iPad than talking face-to-face with my own wife and kids. But that, too, was not beyond diligent spin-doctoring. *I'm a pastor. Caring for the downtrodden is my job, right?*

If you say something to yourself enough times, there's nothing you can't come to believe. I actually had myself convinced I was a good pianist because I'd memorized and could stumble through the theme to Bill Bixby's old TV show, *The Incredible Hulk*. I'd sit in the sanctuary with the lights off and play it for an hour at a time. Honestly, when you're sitting in the dark playing a song titled "The Lonely Man Theme" over and over and don't know why, you … are not … okay.

Now, this may sound like the very bottom of the well, but in truth it's only the first stage of a descent. Self-deception is but the front porch of the "Hotel California." Worse things await.

How Shall We Then Live? Becoming Undeceived

Let's pause, however, before we go to the front desk and check in. In the previous chapter I said this book aims to help the fallen consider the nature of their fall and the unfallen (if there really are any) take warning from it.

So how does one prevent self-deception or, where it has taken root, become undeceived? How does one see truth where one has for so long been insisting on fallacy?

The key problem with self-deception is the "self" part. We are so close to ourselves that we can't recognize when we're doing it. The self-deceived person believes everything is all right, that they aren't drowning. *It's just a bump in the road; it'll pass.* The idea that they should go ask someone else to check their perceptions is out of bounds by definition. The self-deceived are omnipotent and omniscient. If you think you're in need of help, then you're not doing it right.

Self-deception is simply not preventable or correctable by yourself. You need another set of eyes with which to see yourself. This means the only solution is to spend time building good, close relationships with people who are willing to really look at you and tell you what they see.

One of the pastors I respect most in this world has an almost identical story to mine—encountering a person in need, getting too close, texting constantly, heading toward an affair with both feet, just a matter of time. Then one day a friend noticed he'd texted his Lorelai twice just during their conversation. "Jason, what's up with that?" said the friend.

> The only solution is to spend time building good, close relationships with people who are willing to really look at you and tell you what they see.

"Nothing."

But the friend knew Jason well enough to know the difference between nothing and *nothing*. The truth was forced out before anything really bad happened. The church elders got involved. He was rescued and is still a pastor today in a flourishing church community. What saved him? Another set of eyes. A friend saw, recognized what wasn't normal, and got in his face.

That's how it's *supposed* to work. But such defenses have to be built during the good times. You must construct systems of formal and informal accountability when you don't think you really need them. It may be true that you don't need them *yet*, but you will later. Make it a discipline to set up such defenses as a matter of course, independent of what you feel you need, regardless of how strong, healthy, capable, holy, or in control you think you are.

It's not sufficient to have merely concerned bystanders or colleagues. That's what I had. Our church counselor—God bless her—did the best she could, but she wasn't in the right position for it to work. She either believed me because she didn't know me well enough or, disbelieving me, she didn't know how to push upstream against a popular teaching pastor. I wasn't her boss; we had a mutual boss, but high "approval ratings" made anything I said credible.

No, what I'm talking about is a close friend, a spiritual director, a counselor, a mentor, someone who really knows you and your particular brand of BS when they smell it. Someone who won't accept a *nothing* or an *It's fine*. That's what I lacked. In the two years I'd been at that church, I had not cultivated even one relationship for the defense of my own soul. Is it any wonder I lost it?

CHAPTER 2

CROSSING BOUNDARIES

In the little town of Dover, England, famous for its great white cliffs standing high above the sea, two boys spent the afternoon daring each other to complete feats of bravery and skill.

"Climb that tree and jump off that branch," said one. The other did.

"Hit that bird with a stone," said the other. He did.

"Carry that big rock all the way over there and throw it into the ocean ... "

As the day wore on, the tasks grew more daring, till at last one boy drew a line in the dirt with his shoe. "Cross that line!"

The other boy blanched.

"Come on! Step over it. I dare you!"

Still he hesitated.

"Are you chicken? It's just a line."

"Yeah, but—" the other boy stammered—"but you drew it on the very edge of the cliff."

A FEW YEARS BACK, WHILE MIKE PENCE WAS VICE PRESIDENT of the United States, he took a lot of heat for adopting the Billy Graham rule—aka the *Modesto Manifesto*. It was his personal policy never to be alone in the company of a woman other than his wife. I remember having some intellectual sympathy with his critics. "A symptom of a bigger problem," headlined one editorial. After all, this is the twenty-first century. Have we come no further than that? That men and women can't occupy the same social settings without a man feeling sexually tempted? Do we still think women that unsafe—or more accurately, are men really that unsafe around women? Isn't this puritanical and retrogressive?

As I say, I understand this critique. My wife is an IT manager. Ninety percent of the people she works with, supervises, and reports to are men. If each of those men adopted the former veep's approach, she'd do little but sit alone in her office.

Further, Mr. Pence's position grows increasingly unworkable (or at least more complicated) in a world where sexual attraction is less and less defined by gender. Could he insulate himself against all potential sexual pressures and accusations from his own gender as well? It's simply not a viable or fair position to hold. Men need to grow up—and so on.

Again, I very much understand the pushback against the vice president's self-imposed puritanism. How can it possibly work in the wildly pluralistic and over-sexed culture in which we now live?

And Yet ...

And yet my life was destroyed by exactly the sort of relationship Pence so prudishly avoided. How could I blame him? I've seen it firsthand. I've borne in my own body the terrors of a sexualized relationship from which I couldn't free myself ... didn't want to free myself. How much better, happier, more prosperous would so many people's lives be—including my own—if I *had* held to something like Mr. Pence's policy? A sizable part of me says *Feminism be damned. I should have better protected myself and my family.* Progressivism is all well and good till it becomes the vehicle of your own destruction. Then it doesn't seem so progressive.

It may be socially backward for a man to feel the need to defend himself against "womanly wiles," but it is not a groundless fear. Lest you accuse me of one-sidedness, I suspect that in a *#Metoo* world, many women would make similar admissions about protecting themselves from the men in their lives. It sure looks like there are lines out there that—regardless of gender—we should fear to cross, and further, lines that should be defended against those who insist on crossing them.

I want to be especially clear here. Since this book is aimed at people who've already made life-destroying decisions—those who've done the line-crossing—I must focus on the choices I made. The only choices you can control are your own. Those are the ones for which you are responsible. This book must not become a venue where I seek to push blame onto Lorelai. It is a given that she, too, made choices, but I'm not responsible for those. I'm here to own what I did and thereby help others do the same. I intend nothing other than to take full responsibility for the horrors I visited on everyone in my life.

That said, describing the behavior of only one person would give an inadequate picture of what a consensually sexualized relationship looks like. So even at the risk of being misunderstood, I must tell stories. They cast grim lights on us both, but stay focused on the one shining on me. That one reveals the intended lesson.

The YOO-HOO! of a Sexualized Relationship

What do I mean by a sexualized relationship? Is it different from an affair? Yes, it is, though for some it's the stage preceding an affair. It's the point where a colleague, neighbor, or friend starts to become something more. The relationship need not turn physical to be sexualized—mine never did—but it's the process by which two people begin to look for a fulfillment in each other beyond what is appropriate to a colleague, neighbor, or friend.

The sexualized (but not yet physical) relationship might also be considered the first step in an emotional affair—a relationship that contains all the emotional bonding of sexual infidelity, just without the sex.

It's a misty journey from one point to the next. We don't always see it happening in the moment. A story may help clarify this. It would be false to say conversations like this happened *all* the time, but they did happen. This one did.

YOO-HOO! *When are you coming down for coffee?*

Me, dropping tasks, grabbing mug, and heading downstairs to the Keurig machine for a cup of insipid, low-grade, environmentally irresponsible coffee, and then on to the main office of the church where Lorelai works part-time as a front-desk receptionist. Planting myself in the chair in front of her desk, pleasantries are exchanged.

I serve. "What're you up to this weekend?"

She volleys. "Me and my peeps are going dancing at the Mega80's concert downtown on Friday."

"Can I come?"

Now, I don't dance, but it's a little flirty to suggest I do. This is a running joke between us. She, who goes out partying with friends to meet guys nearly every weekend and has since age fifteen, and me, the sedentary homebody who's never contemplated an adventure of that sort in all my sexually repressed days.

"Only if your wife says you can."

Awkward silence.

"So ... an '80s concert?"

"Yeah, they're my fav."

"So ... you, like, dress up in '80s clothes and stuff." Yes, I sound like the high schooler I'm trying to devolve into.

"Well, I do tease my bangs up, but I usually just wear this." Indicates the royal-blue bodycon miniskirt she's wearing. "Except you don't want to wear underwear when dancing."

Silence. *Rockets and sirens going off in my skull.*
"You know, because of the panty line?"
My train of thought violently derails ... many casualties.
"Don't look at me like that. I'm wearing them now, of course.
See?" Stands, turns, and draws finger across offending panty line
on back of skirt.
*Have lost the power to stare at her face. Eyes slide down; eyebrows
slide up.*
She rolls eyes. Sits. "Geez ... men." Smiles coyly.
*Awkward silence. Air crackles with unexpressed sexual tension.
This ... is ... so ... much ... fun!*

Again, I want to be clear. The person in the crosshairs here is me.
Neither of us planned such a conversation. It wasn't premeditated, but I had enough history to know such a display was a possibility. A part of me nurtured a suppressed hope for it. It's partly
why I went down. An itch, a thirst—otherwise understandable,
natural, or at least common to all—but not an itch a coworker is
supposed to scratch.

In a further attempt to stay focused on me, I should add that,
given Lorelai's life story, discussions like this were far more ordinary for her than for me. They did not tantalize her; they were
just her life—her way of being in the world. I will give her that
much benefit of doubt. If there was calculation involved, it is not
my place to judge, at least not here.

For me, on the other hand, her *joie de vivre* was like a hit
of drugs or porn. It opened my imagination to things I'd never
experienced, dulled my senses to the ordinary goods that existed
in my life, generated longings for possibilities and risks my heart
had never contemplated. Her life, despite all its chaos and trouble, became strangely attractive, like the romanticized life of the
Bohemian or dilettante or gypsy.

When I lost my clinician's distance and began imagining
myself in such a life, of course I began to crave it. That's a law

of the human condition—what we dwell on, we begin to desire. The problem isn't the desire, though. Cain's desire for acceptance was natural. His desire for his God was even holy. But he dwelt rather upon the acceptance his brother received from his God till his natural desire raged out of natural boundaries and consumed his soul.

So also with me as I spent hours of unnecessary time in Lorelai's presence, nursing the desire that some of her hypnotic mien might rub off on me. My attentions apparently gave her something she needed as well, and so began a devil's dance between two people who knew they should not dance... yet did.

The thick, dark line that should have stood between us was still there—we never touched or made good on all this sexual tension, but our hearts were already committed. Our souls danced in a circle around the line, never actually crossing it but flirting with it, keeping it between us, constantly rotating till we could not remember which side we were supposed to be standing on—sort of hoping we might land on the same side of it, but of course by accident with deniability and legitimate surprise. "How did we end up in each other's arms? Go figure!"

I will offer no more thoughts on what motivations and agendas may have been present in Lorelai's heart other than to say she saw the danger as well. We talked of it a few times. That, too, was part of the dance. So long as we talked about the pressures openly, we could continue to pretend everything was on the up-and-up. We took our freedom to chat about such improprieties as proof we were keeping appropriate boundaries. If you agree with this rationalization, please go back and reread the previous chapter. You are deceiving yourself.

How Shall We Then Live?
Once You See It, It's Too Late.

So we again come to the question of prevention or correction. What does one do about a sexualized relationship? How do you prevent one from germinating?

This is a hard word that may be fully understandable only to someone who's been through such a relationship, but the ugly truth is by the time you suspect a relationship has become sexualized, it's probably too late. We are sexual creatures. You don't have to do anything special to insert sex into a relationship. It will happen on its own unless special care is taken to prevent it. This is the key. This is, for better or worse, what Mr. Pence was trying to get at.

> You don't have to do anything special to insert sex into a relationship. It will happen on its own unless special care is taken to prevent it.

It begins innocently—with a look over a cup of bad coffee, with an accidentally salacious autocorrect, with an awkward silence, a knowing glance. Somewhere a line is crossed, perhaps inadvertently, perhaps without intent. But the next time you're together, you sense something new is there—a freer tone, a more relaxed atmosphere, less concern about scandal. This all presumes you aren't looking for it. But if you are, then you can sexualize any relationship in no time. It requires no effort; it requires only that you do nothing to stop it.

Said Mel, the cook on the old sit-com *Alice*, "The best defense is a good offense." Live every relationship under the assumption that if you do nothing, the drift of your humanity will be toward sexualization. I'm not telling you to live in fear of sexuality. We were made sexual creatures. Sex is a good. The throbbing feelings that come with sexual flirtations are in themselves good. God made us capable of feeling such things and then bid us be fruitful. But you must not underestimate the effects of the Fall on these good capacities. As fallen creatures, we weaponize our sexuality and use it to destroy ourselves and others. We tantalize ourselves with forbidden fruit and then lament our salivations. We undermine friendship—the noblest of the loves—and pay the price by having nothing left between the sexes but flirtation, lust, and abuse.

If ever there was an insidious peril meant to rouse all our defenses, this potentiality toward sexualization is it.

So draw lines. Look down at them often. Do not make excuses or grant indulgences. It may feel like only butterflies in the stomach, but such flutterings bring forth hurricanes across the oceans of the soul. If I may assume the manner of the apostle John in all his fevered eloquence, *Little children, do not coast with your nature in this, for it has a negative grade, and will betray you.*

But What Then ...

That's all very ominous, to be sure, and if I've done my job, you may already be thinking about a relationship that's become cozier than it ought. What should you do? How do you get out? Or at least how do you reestablish a normalized relationship?

I'm sorry, but I don't know a way to un-sexualize a relationship. They are enchantments easily cast but not easily broken. I can offer only one answer—confess. I'm told it's good for the soul ... even the soul that's lost its sense of direction.

In the early stages, February or thereabouts, recognizing I needed help, I poured out the agony I was feeling to my older brother on the phone—the conflict of both wanting to maintain and wanting to be free of this relationship. To his mind, the only thing to do was make a clean admission of it to the church elders and hope for mercy.

In hindsight, of course, he was right. Had it been discovered at this stage, there would have been hope. Had I confessed it, there would have been mercy. There would have been great efforts by my elders and even the whole congregation to salvage an otherwise effective preaching pastor. It would have been hard, icky, embarrassing ... but I would have survived. I would still be employed. I would still be employable.

Nevertheless, I persisted.

I chose to remain quiet. I chose to believe I could fix it. When I informed Lorelai of my brother's advice, she likewise begged me not to tell "because I'll lose my job," which was not wrong. She was a part-time receptionist, infinitely replaceable. She would pay for both our sin. Well, I couldn't countenance that. She was a single mother of multiple kids with a house in foreclosure, living under accusations of fraud from the welfare office. I'd be a cad to rat her out. So I didn't.

Sir Walter Scott said it best, "Oh, what a tangled web we weave, when first we practice to deceive!"[2] This is equally true when the deception involves simply *not* speaking. Silence is often just as entangling. By silence, we consign ourselves to the next stages of the journey—obsession, regret, and fear.

CHAPTER 3

OBSESSION

Two knights gone a-questing chanced upon a strange pool in a wood. As they approached, they beheld an apparition floating upon the water—a misty vision of the loveliest woman they had ever seen. It hovered there, gazing at them with inviting eyes.

The men stared and stared, till hours later the first knight roused himself and said, "Brother, we have lost half the day gazing upon this phantasm. Let us be gone."

"Nay, brother, just a moment more," said the other.

"'Tis but a mirage."

"Yes, but not the less fair for that."

"You may stay if you wish, but I will away." With that, they parted.

Many years passed, and the first knight had many adventures before he happened again upon that solitary wood. He retraced his steps to the pool and found the spirit hovering above the waters still, lovely as ever.

Of his friend was left nothing but a wasted skeleton, empty eye sockets still transfixed by the beautiful vision.

PILATE ASKED JESUS, "WHAT IS TRUTH?" THAT QUESTION HAS rattled many thinkers throughout the ages. The assumption for most of history was that a statement is *true* if it matches the world *out there.* If I say "The grass is green," and the grass out there is actually green, then I've said something true. (If I say "The grass is brown," and I live in Michigan, that would also be a true statement pretty much all the time.)

In the last few hundred years, however, this rough and workable assumption has been questioned. Is grass *really* green *out there?* Or is "green" only a description of my experience of it, and perhaps it's really a different color *out there.* How would I even know for sure? Do you and I even mean the same thing by "green"?

Truth is apparently more complicated than we thought. We don't simply meet the world as it is; we also have some ability to *shape* the world we're going to inhabit. We can assign different values and meaning to this idea of "green."

I know this is a bit deep and weedy, but it partly explains the phenomenon of obsession—the person who doubles down on a belief that is "obviously" wrong.

Why do our friends of different political, religious, or social stripes so staunchly defend views that appear untrue to us? Often, they are simply grasping different senses of green or doing different things with it. That is not in itself an evil. It may even be a great good, for it means this world is filled with endless possibilities, endless stories to tell one another. We have the power to draw out ever more rich and exciting things from the world with which to bless and challenge other people.

There is, however, an unsettling side to this world-shaping capacity. It means we have the power not only to shape the world into something beautiful but also into something dark and deadly. If we insist on the world being wretched, this will be the world we discover. As C. S. Lewis once wrote of Nature, she is "an accomplished hostess."[3] She will give us whatever we are determined to have from her.

This is why a chapter on obsession follows chapters on self-deception and crossing boundaries. Self-deception is in part the insistence on seeing the world in a way the rest of humanity would not. I may know the falseness of it, but if I insist hard enough, I can act as if that false vision were true and thereby cross boundaries no sane person would cross. Do this long enough, and you will find yourself down Alice's rabbit hole. Because of the world-building role our minds play, if you demand long enough and hard enough that green be blue, it is very likely you will succeed in making yourself color-blind.

"It's My Mind; I'll Think What I Want"

This was what I did. I told myself that certain true things about my life were false and certain false things about Lorelai's life were true. I did it so long and so hard that I came to believe it and even found evidence for it everywhere I looked. Eventually, I lost the capacity to imagine that it had ever been otherwise or to hear when others offered counterevidence.

I reference again that intoxicating conversation with my brother. That little chat was succeeded by a host of others, mostly by email. Here's a (slightly redacted) selection from one I wrote.

I don't know how to let go. I never have. I feel like a bulldog. Once I bite, I never let go. A bulldog will choke and suffocate on what it holds rather than loosen its grip ... even to the point of death. I feel like that. How do I stop wishing, wanting, feeling cheated? How do you stop the nausea of dissatisfaction? And after all the raging is over, and nothing has changed, then what?

I can distract myself with doing things, but like any anodyne, that only works till I figure out it's not getting me any closer to what I want. It's just filler, and then it stops working—and so do I—and I go back to wallowing.

What sort of disorder would produce the following statement: I'd rather be miserable with her, than content without?

That, my friend, is what obsession looks like. It is an early stage, to be sure. You can still hear me fighting. Part of me still wants out. But by definition, we obsess over what we cannot get or retain, so there's no natural point of cessation. You cannot satisfy obsession. It grows like a cancer till it metastasizes and takes over the entire soul. Like the parasitoid wasps that lay their eggs in the body of their fellow insects. The larvae hatch and make a sort of slave-puppet out of the victim while at the same time consuming it from the inside.

Don't believe me? Read this rant of an email to my brother from mere weeks later.

So lest you misunderstand in future, let me speak plainly to my emotional state: I want her—I want her life, her junk, her mind/ soul/body, her history, her oddities and eccentricities, I want her flaws and her problems. I want her laughter and her crying, her poverty and her beauty in their particular qualities—not a rough equivalent! I want to lie down next to her and never rise again. I want to be the last man she ever loves and the first man who really loved her. I want to be that which restores her life and she to be that which restores mine. I want to walk, and eat, and sleep, and work, and play with her every moment in every activity never taking my eyes off her. I want to look her in the eye every day of my life and see the love I see there now, but without the guilt of it feeling illicit and hidden. I want with a Disney-like innocence to "follow my heart" for the FIRST damn time in my life and to hell with the establishment that has bound me my whole life and to which I have meekly submitted like a veal in a box.

The larva has taken over and corrupted the whole mind. Even more, the final line shows that the toxin has begun working backward, poisoning my whole past. Forty years of diligent soul-building in one moment repudiated. None of that wonderful *me* remains. I don't mean I didn't write this nor that I'm not responsible for the drivel it contains. What I mean is that the *me* who wrote it would be unrecognizable to the *me* of just a year earlier. He is unrecognizable to me now. The man who wrote this is a weak, slavering fool, blaming the world for his own choices, crying foul at a game that had actually been pretty good to him. But he can't see it. He's lost. He can no longer recognize his own propaganda.

I wrote it because my brother had expressed some relief that at least I wasn't making claims of having found my soul mate or any such nonsense, so there was some hope I'd be able to escape. I guess I showed him.

His reply, when it came, was succinct—*You are correct. I have greatly erred in my understanding and optimism.*

I had reached the stage of self-destruction where the end has been rendered inevitable, and others had begun to watch with horror-filled eyes. Unchecked obsession will kill you. It knows nothing of proportion or propriety. It is all hunger, thirst, and itch. It is the creeping death, and even now, Cain, it is crouching at your door.

How Shall We Then Live? Living with Obsession

There is no living with obsession. It is deadly by definition. The longer it goes on, the weaker the fighting instinct gets till, like the infected ant, you lie down, consumed from within, and do not rise. If you've been there, you know I speak truth. In fact, it's likely that from this point forward, I am merely describing a hopeless and unchecked fall. We may have left the world of practical advice and possible solutions.

We are merely waiting for the end.

In a sense, I am no longer writing to a person in peril of self-destruction. They can no longer hear me. I am rather reminding those of us who have been there of what it was like so we may shudder inwardly and renew our vows to never return.

To you who are on the path but have not yet met this enemy,

I hope you may be sufficiently frightened to stop where you are and turn around.

Yet it is ungracious of me, I suppose, to assume the obsessed soul is entirely and already lost. So I will yet offer a piece of advice in the hope that mercy will reach you in a way it could not reach me.

One last observation about obsession: Once it has taken hold, gradualism will avail you little.

Though a therapist might disagree, I'm convinced the only hope of breaking obsession's grip is quitting cold turkey. Obsession by nature robs you of the power to exit gradually. My brother, in that very conversation that made me stark raving drunk, expressed the point in all its binary austerity, "Well, it's either you or her. One of you has to go." Once the relationship had become sexualized and I'd become insensible to reason, all remedial halfway measures were worthless. It was time for surgery. No, for amputation. The eye, the hand—they had ceased to be fit luggage for the journey. "Better for you to enter life crippled or lame than with two hands or two feet to be thrown into the eternal fire."[4] I had to either resign or get Lorelai fired. To my brother, it was that simple. I'm ashamed now to admit that he was right. This luggage was too heavy. Dragging it along would kill me. I couldn't take it with me. It had to be left behind.

> The only hope of breaking obsession's grip is cold turkey.

Yet I couldn't. I was sure I knew better. I would control it. I knew I could "just be cool about it." The larvae had taken over. The next stops on the line—fear, depression—were inevitable. They would almost take my life.

CHAPTER 4

REGRET

The drunkard was at the end of his rope. He'd cheated, stolen, and lied his way into life's gutter. With no one left to care and nowhere else to go, he found himself in front of a halfway house. He stumbled through the door and asked for help.

A counselor began intensive therapy, trying to get him to admit his problem. But the man resisted. After a month of stoic evasions and unproductive circling, the alcoholic finally put his head into his hands and burst into tears.

"I wish ... I wish ..." he mumbled.

The therapist leaned in, anticipating the breakthrough. "What do you wish?"

"I wish I'd bought better Scotch."

EVERYONE HAS REGRETS. EVERYONE LOOKS BACK AT THE long list of choices they've made in life and says of various ones either *Well played* or *What was I thinking?* Life is a choose-your-own-adventure book but with the exception that you don't get to go back to the beginning and take a different route. Neither can you peek ahead at the various outcomes and then decide which page to turn to. In our best moments, we analyze and predict, but many of our most defining choices happen in real time—in the heat of lust, the throes of rage, or the fog of fear. They're not planned and always look different on Monday morning. Much of the time we shrug our shoulders, mumble, "Well, that could've gone better," and get on with life. Some choices, however, cling to us like a sick odor. Some get dragged around with us like a cat on a leash. Some regrets become the material of new bad choices.

This means regrets are not all alike. Later, I'll talk about real legitimate regret—the kind you must live with *after* you've screwed up and hurt a bunch of people. That sort is particularly heavy and in some sense is a just desert—a merited consequence we must learn to bear with constancy. But that's not what's on the table here.

I'm interested in the role regret plays in the run-up to self-destruction. For the sake of contrast, I'm tempted to call it false or illegitimate regret, but that would be imprecise. The feelings of regret are real enough. Choices get made because of them, but they're false insofar as they flow out of self-deception and obsession.

These are not the regrets of having done wrong but regrets about opportunities not taken. The sort of regret that makes you think of your life as a failure or as characterized by a lack of self-actualization. *Self-actualization*, that psycho-babbly word responsible for so much evil in the world. We can justify anything and everything on the basis of it. Under its bewitchment, we will ditch longstanding marriages, welch on responsibilities to children and aging parents, cheat in business, pile on debt, and bounce from broken relationship to broken relationship searching for that authentic life implied by the meme, "You do you."

Regret is one of the key and necessary elements for generating the sense of injury by which we justify casting off those to whom we have long-standing responsibilities.

Regretting Success

It doesn't take a psychotherapist to foresee the trajectory of the person determined to void every good they've known in order to justify some hideous fantasy of self-actualization. *False* regret will become one's traveling companion on the downhill journey toward *real* regret. To speak of my case with brutal bluntness, I talked myself into regrets I had no right to have.

My poor brother, forced to put up with my droning nonsense. Is there any greater act of love than to listen without judgment to a loved one diligently scattering manure about their life just so they can feel justified in raging, "I deserve better than this!"? I was a successful professional with an earned PhD and rapidly expanding public platform. I had a beautiful family and a fairly secure upper-middle-class life. My situation would be the envy of the masses—and still I wrote,

> *The details don't really matter, but it seems that, having rooted through my whole history, upbringing, love life, and marriage, my therapist is convinced I suffer from deep and unresolved regrets over having married Denise, which I did out of a sense of obligation and a following of "the rules" and not out of any real passion or love. That I have lived my whole life being "the good boy" and submitting to systems of behavior I didn't choose and are contrary to my instinctive "more passionate" nature.*
>
> *And now I'm basically exploding on the inside because I've reached the age (mid-life?) where I'm realizing I've gone too far down my particular road to ever make the changes that will bring me into the kind of happiness I've always wanted—wanted, but have denied myself so to be "a good boy" and follow "the rules." It explains so much of my life.*

The part of this rant that's true—it wouldn't have been compelling unless it had *some* truth in it—is that I actually *had* followed a pretty straight and narrow path through my life. I wasn't a party kid in high school or college. I never snuck out of the house at night, never met a girl on the sly, don't remember ever being grounded. The first alcohol I ever consumed was at age twenty-two on my wedding night—a night of several firsts for me. The worst thing I probably ever did was pull the fire alarm in high school on the last day of my senior year and then play dumb when the principal called me into his office. Or maybe in college, when my dorm mates and I broke into the college chapel and had a toga party on stage complete with candles and a mock séance, wherein we tried to summon the spirit of Eric Clapton, who did not appear because … well, he was still alive.

I went straight from Bible college to seminary and on from there, in an unbroken ascent, to Christian ministry. I honestly don't think my parents lost an hour of sleep over me at any stage. I was the poster child for the intergenerational transfer of evangelical *sticky* faith. And my reward had been commensurate with my stewardship.

I don't say this with anything like self-congratulation. This was actually the problem. In the throes of my obsession, I was regretting never having sown wild oats, gone on a *Rumspringa*, or "aimed to misbehave." Even now looking back on it as a regret, I think there's some small truth there. Part of being young involves the embrace of risk. It's the time of life designed for it, the manner in which we become our own person. It's one reason the military recruits eighteen-year-olds—they're up for adventure and not very good at calculating risk.

So if I had legitimate regrets about roads not taken, I should have been laying them in the balance next to all the icky things I'd avoided through "clean living."

For example, while I'd "missed out" on teenage promiscuity, I also skipped being a teenage father, having a substance addiction or STD, and encountering a host of other possibilities that often accompany that sort of youthful risk.

I "missed out" on the drunken party stage of my youth, yes,

but as a result, I had a whole set of different adventures—trips to Russia, Ukraine, Ireland, the Caribbean, and all over the US. Acceptance into a prestigious PhD program on a full ride that didn't even require me to relocate or change jobs. Homeownership. Healthy children.

Even in the days just before it all came apart, I could have seen myself as on the verge of great professional adventure. At forty, there's still lots of time for a new thing. New risks! If I wanted some danger, I could go jump out of a perfectly good airplane!

Today, it's obvious to me that I'd been more than adequately compensated for anything I missed by taking the straight and narrow. And for the average regret, such observations should've been more than sufficient to bring me to terms with life and move on. When coupled with obsession, however, such small regrets become all-absorbing. In the throes of self-deception, they get reinterpreted as evidence of an inauthentic self.

When the obsessed me laid all that asceticism next to Lorelai's footloose, Kevin-Bacon-dancing-in-a-warehouse life … well, even now, I hardly knew what it was I was pining for. I had no words for it, had never wanted that life, had never even imagined it … till that moment.

Even watching her struggle under the addictions, impoverishments, and debilitations such a life inevitably entails, I could not bring myself to see anything but how *authentically* she threw herself into it … and I envied that authenticity.

It was as though I, the older brother, had followed my younger brother into that far country to watch him waste our father's wealth in prodigality, and even knowing the pigsty was coming for him, I envied him nonetheless—not so much jealous of his wine and his women as his gall and his gumption. He had the defiant cheek to cast off societal norms and restraints and simply *be*. I had always been a human *doing* and felt I was for the first time in the presence of a human *being*. I can hardly explain the attraction, as of a force, like heavy gravity, warping my universe so that I was now spinning uncontrollably toward a gravitational depression in the middle. And what a depression it would be.

How Shall We Then Live? Dealing with Regret

Regret has one straightforward solution. Obvious, really. *Contentment.* At least contentment is the opposite of regret and therefore, like an element of medieval alchemy, its antidote. And it appears to be a virtue that can be acquired. At least, the apostle Paul claimed to have *learned* to be content in all manner of situations.[5] Under normal conditions, I assume contentment is obtained like all other virtues—through the building of good habits of the soul.

> Regret has one straight forward solution— Contentment.

But these are not normal conditions. How does the *obsessed* mind learn contentment? I confess, I don't know. Obsession by definition obsesses. It knows nothing of temperance, discretion, or "good habits of the soul." Obsessed people do not diet—they bloat or starve. They are the patron saints of repetitive stress fractures, carpel tunnel syndrome, and Netflix binges. You find them at the extremes. Ask any alcoholic or drug addict. Obsessed people can *only* regret, and the regret facilitated by obsession becomes material for new and greater regrets. As Grandpa Simpson said when found wringing his hands in a porta potty, "This elevator only goes to the basement, and someone made an awful mess down there." The elevator of obsession goes only one direction.

Under such conditions, contentment cannot be *learned* as Paul suggests. All the habits of the soul run the opposite direction. The very will has become a citadel against it. The power of learning virtue has been lost. This is consistent with both my own experience and what I have watched happen in others. We are not as strong as we think we are.

My only real advice for the obsessed regret-er who can no

longer learn contentment—indeed your only hope—is to confess. Wake up! Come clean to your family, your boss, your pastor, your counselor. Confess, and perhaps you will receive mercy—from God and others. Perhaps amid the shock of telling yourself and others the truth of your situation, God will meet you with an unexpected gift of contentment—a contentment you could not yourself choose. Otherwise, by the time you've reached this stage of the journey, self-destruction is nearly assured. Cain is even now searching for the rock with which he will end his brother's life ... and his own.

CHAPTER 5

FEAR

She shot out of her chair as the smoke detector began to shriek. Then she smelled it. She ran into the living room to find her eight-year-old standing before the couch, which was now a ball of fire. She grabbed the extinguisher, and in a minute the conflagration was reduced to an ashy, foul-smelling mess. Looking around at the blackened rug, walls, and ceiling, she noticed that her son was holding a box of matches.

"You did this? Why?"

"I was afraid you'd yell at me for spilling jam on the couch."

"So you set it on fire? What on earth possessed you to—"

"I told you—I was afraid!"

VERY EARLY ON, I BEGAN TO WONDER IF I WAS IN TROUBLE. Doubt continued to whisper that this relationship wasn't really on the up-and-up. I knew I had good and noble reasons for wanting to help this troubled soul, but I also sensed that something else was starting to gum up my soul's machinery.

Despite my best efforts at self-deception, some part of me recognized that the choices I was making were not the sort of choices I would have made even six months earlier. The reasons may have been stuffed like a Thanksgiving turkey (and in roughly the same manner), but the choices themselves were on display before my eyes.

Incoming text: YOO-HOO! *When are you coming down for coffee?*

My answer—Now! And with unreasonable haste.

This daily rush downstairs with mug in hand disquieted me somewhere on the inside, like how indigestion augurs an ulcer. You can ignore it but not really deny it. Your stomach does in fact hurt.

So more out of a mechanically trained response than any true awareness of my peril, I decided to sound out some wise counsel. I tracked down a local pastor who was also a spiritual director— more than this, a director of spiritual directors and a seasoned pastor and administrative functionary in his denomination—the very person to understand my dilemma.

A week later I sat in his office talking about the malaise creeping over my life. Mere minutes later, and not by intention, I found myself in tears talking about the strange bondage I was experiencing with Lorelai—the conflicted tug toward going deeper in and the equally strong desire to be free. When I finished pouring out my gray agony, I looked to him hoping he would say something that would give me a way of getting out of the hole I was in.

His response was something like, "Well, I can only tell you what would happen if you were part of our denomination. Pending a review of all these texts and conversations, you'd most certainly be terminated and never pastor in one of our churches again. But since you're not in this denomination, I can only suggest that you confess to your elders and take your just deserts." To be fair to him, I don't know if that's actually what he said, but in the state of mind I was in, that's what I heard.

My despair was so great that all I could think to say was, "Well, I suppose pastors in your denomination have learned to hide their problems pretty well, then." There's a lot of snark in that comment, I admit, but that doesn't make it false. Even now in hindsight, a good part of me thinks what I said bears examination. But what I want to highlight now is how that response reflected a new step in my degradation.

It was a sort of wake-up call, but in the wrong direction. I was entering a new stage. From that moment, fear would play a central role in my story. I became afraid—afraid to continue, afraid to turn back, afraid to speak up, afraid to remain silent. I was afraid of Denise, afraid of Lorelai, afraid of my elders, afraid of myself.

I now realized that, no matter how strong my desire to fix things, I was too far gone for them to be fixed. A trail of texts would show my complicity. I was already lost. If I breathed a word of it, I would lose everything. There was no escape. I had sprung the trap on myself. I had sought the sympathetic ear of a stranger, and in a heartbeat he had cut through all the self-deception and obsession and told me the truth of my position. The disease was terminal.

My woeful state may be best seen in the fact that I managed to feel outrage at the situation—as if I'd had no contributing hand in it. Like the mouse, having freely eaten the crumbs it knew all along were poisoned, now in its death throes, wasting its final breaths on imprecations against the farmer.

My mind spun like an overworked hard drive.

It wasn't my fault.

It was all my fault.

Fault was irrelevant. I was a dead man, walking. It was just a matter of time till it all came out.

After this, I emailed my brother in a fit of animal rage over what now seemed the inevitable, inescapable end of the whole ... well, affair.

If I were to act on this [have an actual physical affair with Lorelai], *I lose everything immediately and dramatically; if I deny it, I will lose all anyway, but slowly and cancerously. What then will rebellion cost that I will not lose anyway? God has taken from me my desire for Denise, but left her here. God has now taken [Lorelai] from me, but left the desire for her. Heal from that? Not in one lifetime.*

I will end by quoting [Lorelai] on the day we discovered these facts (which is likewise the day we also knew we had to begin stepping away from each other). She texted: "I can't seem to make you hate me! I sense from you a kind of unconditional love I have never known before from anyone—and now it's forbidden? What the F**K is God doing?!!"

That, dearest brother, is so exquisitely right.

Rage is a short-term defense against fear.

Rage is the soul shouting itself hoarse.

But inevitably, once the voice gives out, the creeping fear will have its way with you.

Fear makes everything worse. It clouds the mind, threatens the sanity, paralyzes the will. There is nothing redemptive or holy about fear, nothing from God in it. It is all darting eyes, looking over shoulders, and shredding documents. It makes us hide from the very people who would try to save us if they only knew. It turns every friend into an informant, makes every incidental glance into a threat, makes every casual observation suspicious. My mind continued to spin. People knew everything. People knew nothing. People, with their constantly probing eyes, were now my enemies.

As a general rule, these are not thoughts conducive to pastoral ministry. Most people would not describe their pastor as the person trying to hide in plain sight. And pastors have it worse than many on this score. They are, above all people, observed, watched, scrutinized.

They also have more to fear from dissection than most. If an accountant or a mechanic has an affair, he may lose his marriage, and maybe his family, but he'll probably keep his job, his friends, his broader public reputation. A pastor, a missionary, a Christian schoolteacher or administrator, however ... well, you can hear it for yourself in another of those frothing emails to my sibling. Note I'm not so angry here. Rage has passed. My soul is now hoarse. Now you can hear the fear plainly as it slides toward insensible resignation.

> *And unlike "normal" people, if my marriage fails I also lose my job, career, home, income earning potential, reputation, plus I devastate the lives of hundreds of parishioners. This shill has NO choice but keep playing the game.*
>
> *God, I'm so miserable ... and I still have to live half my life yet.*
>
> *I'm just venting here; there's nothing for you to do. I'm not even asking you to pray, cuz I don't know what good that'll do. Prayer just gives the illusion of progress till you figure out that it doesn't change anything that really matters.*
>
> *If God exists, the only form of Christianity that adequately explains him is Deism, for he manages the universe as if he were not there at all. And a silent God is worse than a mythical one because it means he exists but doesn't care.*
>
> *Well, thanks for listening to ol' Prometheus groan in his chains ...*

Ah yes, Prometheus, the Greek titan who defied the gods by stealing fire and bequeathing it to humanity, thereby becoming the father of cultural progress. Yet as punishment for this act, he was chained to a rock where each day Zeus's eagle was sent to feed on his liver, which would then grow back overnight to be devoured again the next day. Ever living, ever suffering. I was haunted by the myth. I had printed out full-color images of Lair's, Ruben's, and Mikhailov's paintings of the tragic myth and hung them on the wall of my office at the church—an unsettling cry for help, I now suppose.

Then came the wintry weekend when I was supposed to drive up to a little camp in northern Michigan, where the church elders were sequestered for a planning retreat. It was being run by the lead pastor (I was "only" the part-time preaching pastor who reported to the lead), but they'd asked me to come up and lead a session of worship and prayer.

I began the drive with the shade of Prometheus heavy upon me, pondering a line from the well-known worship song that talks about my end drawing near and my time having come.[6] The song's intention is to express the comfort the Christian has even in death, but for me it had become a ponderous and weighty curse. The end of all things snapped at my heels like the wolves in the opening of Jack London's *White Fang*. There was no peace in life, nor confidence in death, only lingering dread. A slow thudding of years upon the soul like the roar of the surf, deadening all joy, darkening all skies, water wearing down the rock a century at a time. A man forty years in, only halfway through his life, wishing he could die right then and be spared the certainty of coming shame.

I was approaching the junction of 10 Mile Road and Michigan 37. The snow had made the roads treacherous. In those days I drove a little fast, a little reckless. I hit the brakes for the stop light. The car started to slide. I looked up to see an eighteen-wheeler hurtling full throttle up to the intersection on the crossroad.

My foot eased off the brake as time slowed. The brain is capable of an infinite number of thoughts in such moments. I realized if I just pulled my foot off the brake, the timing of that truck would prove a convenient solution to all my troubles. It would be tragic, but people remember tragic heroes with fondness. There would be no shame. The dark story would never be told. I would exit this world at the height of admiration, honored as an incidental casualty of the weather. There would be a scholarship at the seminary named after me, a plaque on the church's wall. It wouldn't even be considered a death by ... I didn't think the word *suicide*. My foot eased further off the brake, my decision mostly made.

In that eternal second of time when the happiest possible future for me lay out there on the snowy ground under a police tarp, a memory surged over me unbidden with an ammoniac sharpness that froze what was to be my final breath.

A birthing ward in Butterworth Hospital in downtown Grand Rapids. A nurse laying a small antiseptic-smelling bundle in my terrified arms. A small round face turned toward me with startlingly blue eyes. An impossible glimmer of recognition. A smile. My world unmade.

Then the vague impression of that same child making her way in the world ... fatherless.

This takes so many words to record, but in real time it was all done in about a second and a half. My foot slammed down. The inventor of anti-lock brakes earned his angelic wings. The truck rushed by at 60 mph, horn blaring, throwing slush onto my windshield.

I sat for a long time on the empty road.

I wish I could say this moment altered my course. It did not. I was back on script now, but with a new reason for dread. My daughter would keep her father ... and see him disgraced. Had I even done her a favor by stopping?

Numbness began to accrete itself once again onto my soul like barnacles on a ship. Eventually, the torpor of the damned flowed back into all the crevices. I shed not a tear. I was a machine about to do a machine's work. I turned right and proceeded to the camp, where I led my elders in a hell of a solo worship set—not hard to do when you're already in hell.

The elders talked about that time of worship for months— "So authentic, so real." I, of course, knew it for what it really was—the emotional hangover of suicidal ideation poured back into "the job." Yes, I was now back on script again. My stage skills were as strong as ever. It was only my soul I'd left like a corpse on the highway back at 10 Mile and M-37.

CHAPTER 6

DEPRESSION

A traveler walking through the hill country was overtaken by night, which rolled toward him with unexpected suddenness. He saw the lights of a farmhouse in the distance. Approaching, he found the old farmer sitting on the stoop, sharpening his sheep shears.

"Excuse me, sir," said the traveler. "I don't know what to do. The night has come."

"So you be looking for a place to flop, then?"

"Thank you, no. I am in a great hurry." Then looking around at the gathering darkness, he sighed with resignation. "But I suppose I will have to await the morning."

The old farmer shrugged. "Well, if it's the morning you're seeking, stopping here isn't the fastest way to find it."

"No?"

"No, fastest way to morning is to keep walking just as you were ... that way ... into the dark."

THREE MONTHS FROM SELF-DECEPTION TO DESPAIR. THAT'S all it took. Rather than wake me up, that close-up view of semi-truck tires had hardened me. As I saw it, the event changed none of the facts, created no new opportunities, gave no hope.

But I now knew I couldn't take the easy way out, and that itself became a new source of misery.

I settled into a rigorous and methodical despair. I was already dead. I was just waiting for the rest of the world to realize it. The mechanics of my job took over. I translated Greek, shambled to staff meetings, taught theology, graded papers, wrote sermons ... and waited for the end.

Every day Zeus's eagle came in the form of a text. YOO-HOO! *When are you coming down for coffee?* I no longer leapt up with eagerness. Now I rose slowly, ponderously, inevitably, descending the stairs like water flowing into a dark cave.

So Many Kinds of Depression

I'm told by people who know such things that depression can be rooted in all sorts of events and situations—a traumatic past, a stressful present, a hopeless future. I'm told there are strong neuro-chemical causes or at least contributors. Some people struggle with it perpetually, some cyclically, and for others it flares up only when aggravated by certain situations.

Then there's a depression like mine—one that grows out of constantly lying to yourself, pining for things you don't have, raging against a world that has withheld some tasty morsel you see others all around you eating ... or suspect they are. Not all depression comes from without, feeling causeless, like a disease. Sometimes it's self-inflicted, like a gunshot wound.

This, I've often heard, is what's going on in the story of King Ahab. He wants to buy Naboth's family vineyard. Naboth doesn't want to sell. "And Ahab went into his house vexed and sullen because of what Naboth the Jezreelite had said to him ... And he lay down on his bed and turned away his face and would eat no food."[7] I disagree. This is not depression; this is merely a tantrum. Where the observation about Ahab's depression becomes valuable is realizing that some depressions do *start* this way. Mine did. Perhaps the only reason Ahab's disappointment didn't turn into full-blown depression was that his wife was more screwed up than he was. Jezebel simply had Naboth executed on trumped-up charges and his property transferred to the crown. If I'm any judge of the journey, however, Jezebel only coolly did what self-deception, obsession, and depression would have eventually brought the fevered Ahab to do on his own. Many roads lead to the bottom, and, sadly, sometimes we have help on the way.

The point is that this isn't how it's supposed to go down. Disappointments in life are common, meaning both that they're frequent and that they happen to everybody. When we meet one, we're supposed to engage in reasonable mourning and then move on. Easy come, easy go—it's the only way to endure something as absurd as life. Sometimes, however, a disappointment gets stuck crosswise in us and makes it hard to move on. Instead, we dwell on it—like Ahab, like Cain. We rehearse it endlessly. We drive it deeper down into our soul than it deserves to be. We marinate in it. Steep like a tea bag. We don't learn any grace or resilience from it; we merely brine.

In such a case you may very well induce your own depression. It's the easiest, most natural thing in the world for a self-deceived, fear-filled person to move from a disappointment to a life-threatening mental state.

To Me Depression Tastes Like ...

All that self-recriminating stuff said, depression of any sort can bring a person to ruination. If you're enduring it, you're in danger of a life-destroying choice. So regardless of how you got there, you need to know a few of the things I've learned.

I don't write as a physician or a therapist. I write as someone who has endured. That is what I have to offer to the conversation.

C. S. Lewis made the observation (which I'll update a touch) that if you want to know what *being in love* is, you can ask either a psychologist or a pair of lovers.[8] Both will give you true answers, but they will be different answers. One will tell you what it's like from the outside—raised blood pressure, pupil dilation, and increased pheromones. The other will speak of it from within— the rending of the heart, the eternality of the promises, the desire to sit and stare at the beloved. The issue comes down to what sort of answers you're looking for. Both have value, but they are not interchangeable. If you want a clinical examination of depression, go read one of the wonderful books on it by the experts. I'm talking about what it feels like from the inside.

Denise had been telling me my color was off for more than a month. I was getting up every night around 2:00 a.m. to go lie on the living room floor and "pray," which was code for weep and scream at God for … what? Not giving me what I wanted? Not helping me find a way out of the trap? Both actually, sometimes at the same time.

Self-deception and obsession had run their course, and I was in a bad way. I was depressed and didn't know it. Later I would read Jerry Sittser's description of depression and recognize myself in it.

> I found depression completely debilitating. It took Herculean strength for me to get out of bed in the morning. I was fatigued all day long, yet at night I was sleepless. I would lie awake by the hour, feeling the torment of a darkness that no one could see but me. I had trouble concentrating. I was apathetic and desireless. I could not taste food, see beauty, or touch anything with pleasure. I exacerbated the problem by telling virtually no one about my struggle. Friends and colleagues marveled at how well I was doing. But inside I was a living dead man.[9]

A living dead man—that was me. Unable to speak, unable to

see or hear, unable to even respond to life. Gears continued to click through the day's activities, but I was a mere automaton, running, running, running, day and night. No real life in me.

If you've ever tried to encourage a person who's in the throes of depression, you know it's like telling a blind man how beautiful the painting on the wall is. He just can't see it. Depression destroys your ability to see and hear truth. The whole internal life is consumed by a silent scream that need not pause for breath, a soulish, Cain-like bellowing that drowns out both reason and imagination.

Christian Advice Misreads Depression ... Except When It Doesn't.

One misconception that floats around the church is that depression is inconsistent with faith. Therefore, if you're depressed, the cause must be a lack of faith. It might even be sin. Therefore, the solution must be to repent your sin and have faith, and then it'll go away. I'm told by experts who study such things that this isn't really how depression works. Depression is often rooted in chemistry, sensitivity, trauma, or other issues unrelated to the person's capacity to "believe in things." As such, the sin-centered explanation seems to me a bit tone-deaf.

In my case, however, I have to pause. What if I *had* repented? What if I *had* spoken up and confessed? If I had opened my clenched fist and released the rock that was dragging me into the deep, what then? Would *my* depression have lifted? Can the "tone-deaf" interpretation be right on the statistical margin? And if it can, is it only my pride keeping me from seeing the main point—that, yes, it is wrong in almost every case ... but not in mine?

If the idiot you least liked and respected gave you a piece of advice that was actually sound and would save you from great sorrow, would you refuse to take it out of spite? If *my* depression *was* actually self-induced through a fondling of evil and obsessing over falsehoods, then wouldn't the right choice—the spiritually mature choice—have been to heed the warning of even the person I considered spiritually anemic? After all, *I* was the one on the cusp of destroying all things. Their sin, if it is a sin to say such things, was mere callowness and infantilism. Mine arose out of actual vice and corruption. Who, then, ought to be listening to whom?

Take it as an inviolable principle of spiritual math that if you've reached a point where the voices of Christianity you think most shallow are actually speaking truth you need to hear ... you're almost at the bottom.

How Shall We Then Live?
Is There No Comfort?

All that said, depression of any kind is wicked awful. Regardless of whether you've arrived there by the physical-chemical route or, like me, through self-induced lunacy, the darkness is just as great. And it seems to me that depressed people of every stripe tell themselves a particular lie. This lie doesn't constitute a self-deception as discussed earlier; rather, it is a lie that in part makes depression what it is. If you don't believe it, you aren't depressed, and if you could manage to disbelieve it, your depression would ease or dissipate.

The lie is *You are all alone.*

The corresponding truth is *No, you are not.*

To be clear, I don't intend to make you *feel* less alone by offering a bunch of affirmations of your worth. No, I'm pointing out two objective senses in which you are just not as alone as you think you are. I don't know if they'll help; they may not make you *feel* any better, and I don't offer them for that reason. Feelings and facts generally don't give two hoots what the other is saying, especially during the midnight of depression. I say these are *facts* insofar as they are truths, and as such I'm offering them to your brain, to your sense of reason. Your feelings don't change them, although they may prevent you from accepting them. Nevertheless, store them away so that when the need arises, you can trot them out and ponder them.

More People Care More Than You Think They Do

Almost no one is as alone as they feel. From the hormonally overwhelmed middle schooler to the middle-aged single adult sitting in their apartment every Friday night, most of us have more people in our life than we think. Cain himself had parents who presumably cared about him—not perfect parents, to be sure, but people who knew something of loss. Cain was not alone in his despair. He just believed the lie—and his children have been doing it ever since.

It is true that most of the people who surround you are busy about their own lives and not thinking about you right now, but it is also true many of those same people would happily sit over coffee and listen to you reflect on your life if they only knew you were struggling. Remember, they're just ordinary people with their own struggles with work, kids, debt, and overdue library books, so don't expect therapy from them. That's what a therapist is for.

But you'd be surprised how many of your friends and acquaintances, with but a little coaching, would be more than willing to sit with you on your ash heap in silence for an hour if they understood that's all they were being asked to do. What scares people away isn't the fact that you're depressed but that they feel out of their depth in your bottomless pool of grief. They think they have to be *helpful*. Let them know up front that you don't need them to fix anything. You just need them to be present and listen.

Even my most tangential of friends are sufficiently decent to listen graciously if I tell them in advance that this is all I need—just to listen to me. Often simply spending time with someone is enough to stave off the worst of despair for a while.

What's true of most of our friends is even truer of the few people in our lives who deeply care what happens to us. A central feature of depression is being convinced that spouses, parents, adult children, or siblings don't really care.

But they do.

They can see the hunted horror in your expression. They've watched the circles grow dark under your eyes. They're concerned —frightened, even—but they don't know what to say or how to enter your darkness. They would be there in a minute—even from across the city or the state—if they thought it would help.

They would enter your silence if you could just find the strength or courage to invite them in, if they knew they were welcome and that their presence wouldn't disturb your sorrows. Yes, there's the rub, isn't it? I know the darkness in which you walk, and the possibility of speaking to someone else about it seems pointless or beyond your strength. You don't think you can ask for help. But this lethargy regarding what others have to offer betrays a misunderstanding of your real need.

You are not looking for people to help you **You don't *fix*** *fix* the depression. No, you don't *fix* depres-**depression;** sion; you *outlast* it. It must simply be endured. **you *outlast* it.** You have to survive it. You have to not lie down and give up. Most people, who would be rightly terrified at having to say something that would fix your depression, would be relieved to a fever pitch to discover all you really want from them is silent companionship. You need help enduring. That is a modest need.

The simple company of average people is often more than sufficient to give us the strength to endure. You'd be surprised how often otherwise common and ordinary people become extraordinary resources for endurance—through watching cheesy movies; over bad cups of coffee or lukewarm beers; by wasting time over video games, a cookbook, a puzzle; or just sitting on a bench in the park watching their children play, especially if you don't have kids of your own. Play the long game. Stop trying to outsprint the depression. Just walk. Walk *with* someone, doing something common, earthy, and frivolous that has nothing to do with depression. Then tomorrow, do it again. Maybe you should put this book down and go call one of these average, extraordinary people right now.

You're Already Part of the Longest Game

Part of what makes depression so horrible is the overwhelming sense that you're the first, last, and only person to ever feel this way. A moment's thought will tell you this can't be true, but it *feels* true, and that is enough to wreck your life. So again, ignoring your feelings for a moment, I want to demonstrate for your thinking mind the falseness of the idea. Then when your brain is ready to listen, you'll have been forearmed.

Read the following prayer from a journal—it's not mine. Ask yourself what sort of lost, broken, backslidden Christian would write such a thing.

> *Lord, my God, who am I that You should forsake me? The child of your love—and now become the most hated one—the one You have thrown away as unwanted—unloved. I call, I cling, I want—and there is no One to answer—no One on Whom I can cling—no, No One.—Alone ... Where is my faith?—even deep down, right in, there is nothing, but emptiness & darkness.—My God—how painful is this unknown pain...I have no faith.— I dare not utter the words & thoughts that crowd in my heart—& make me suffer untold agony.*[10]

This seems to play right into the hands of the churchly misunderstanding mentioned above. Of course this person suffers so—where is her faith? Where is her victorious confidence? Where is the claiming of the promises? No saint this! Surely some member of the poor uneducated unwashed masses of second-rate occasional once-a-month Christians. Probably doesn't even lift her hands to the worship choruses at church, or pray against the spirits of depression, or repost inspirational Facebook memes. No wonder she's depressed. She's not keeping up on any of the pious Christian busyness that's supposed to somehow prevent us from having "blue periods."

Well, you're partly right. She wasn't doing any of these. She was busy holding the hands of the dying in Calcutta, India.

This is from the journal of Mother Teresa.

In contrast to the fast-food spirituality that dominates much of contemporary Christianity, telling us our sorrows are signs of spiritual deficiency, the historic voice of the Christian church says something quite different.

It says *You are not alone.*

The greatest men and women of the faith have walked in the darkness in which you now find yourself. I could give you a dozen great voices from the history of the church who've written on it—St. John of the Cross, Thomas à Kempis, Brother Lawrence, Thomas Merton. And their pedigree goes even further back—back to David writing psalmic laments and Elijah broken and hiding in a cave.

If you get nothing else out of this chapter, get this. You wander, yes, but you are not lost. Too many others have walked here before you and assure us such seasons of darkness are par for the course. Though you cannot see them for the darkness, you are surrounded by the church of all times in all places. The greatest saints of history cry out to you from their desert caves, their monasteries and sickbeds, from the ghettos and the forgotten places of the world. Their fingers reach out to you in darkness to hold your hand, dry your sweaty brow, and whisper to you, *We know, we know, we understand. The darkness is real, but you are not alone and this is not the end.* A great cloud of witnesses testifies to you that this dark journey you're on is common, survivable, and even pregnant with possible glory.

Do not forget—our Lord himself once lay upon his face in the darkness of a garden and in anguish asked his Father in heaven, "Are you really going to do it this way?" And the silent answer was "Yes. By means of the great darkness of a cross and the great silence of a tomb, I will save the world." And Jesus's response to the darkness makes all the difference—"So be it." Do you hear the exhalation, the rest, the release, the enduring trust?

No, you do not fix darkness. You outlast it. You endure, and the enduring changes you. Many precious things grow only in dark places. One final thought from Jerry Sittser on the grace we learn only from walking in the dark places.

> Though I experienced death, I also experienced life in ways that I never thought possible before—not after the darkness, as we might suppose, but *in* the darkness. I did not go through pain and come out the other side; instead, I lived in it and found within that pain the grace to survive and eventually grow. I did not get over the loss of my loved ones; rather, I absorbed the loss into my life, like soil receives decaying matter, till it became a part of who I am. Sorrow took up permanent residence in my soul and enlarged it. I learned gradually that the deeper we plunge into suffering, the deeper we can enter into a new, and different, life—a life no worse than before and sometimes better. A willingness to face the loss and to enter into the darkness is the first step we must take. Like all first steps, it is probably the most difficult and takes the most time.[11]

Stop trying to outrun the darkness. You can't. It pursues with the unrelenting progress of a whole world turning toward night.

But there's the key. The shortest way to morning is straight ahead into the darkness. If the sun is ever to rise again, it will be in that direction. So get up and start walking. Endure. Let the darkness do its soul-expanding work. Walk, rest, sleep, repeat. That is enough for now.

CHAPTER 7

Running on Empty

A lawyer was feeling a bit blue down in her soul. She'd just won the biggest case of her career, and her name was on everyone's lips. Her business was on the cusp of a major expansion, and every dream she'd ever had seemed about to come true. And yet, despite all this, she felt a curious disquiet building in her soul. The color seemed to be bleeding slowly out of her world, and she didn't know why. So she called up a colleague who was a therapist and told him what she was feeling.

"No, you're not depressed," he said.

"I'm not? How can you tell?"

"Are you calling from the office?"

"Yes."

"So you went to work today?"

"Yes."

"Then you're not depressed."

"But how does all that mean I'm not depressed?"

"You're still functioning."

THESE LITTLE PARABLES AT THE BEGINNING OF EACH CHAPTER are usually fictitious. I include them as a sort of mental preparation for the subject. This chapter, however, is headed with a partly true story. Before I went to the spiritual director and discovered fear, before I nearly spread myself over the intersection of 10 Mile and M-37, even before Lorelai and I looked each other in the eye the first time and saw that first leering glint of sexual tension, before all of that ... I was already tired.

In the previous two years, I had completed a PhD, taken on a pastorate while continuing to teach full time at the seminary, written two books, welcomed our fourth child, and was up for promotion from assistant to associate professor. I was a high-functioning professional.

What I was *not* doing, however, was taking Sabbath rest, investing in my marriage, or maintaining patterns of recreation and exercise. Frankly, I had become a bit of a machine before Lorelai showed up at the church office and poured sugar in my gas tank. I was tired.

So just about the same time Lorelai and I were settling into a coffee routine, I sat down with a counseling colleague at the seminary and told him I thought I might be depressed. The conversation proceeded much as in the parable above. I had, it was true, just come through the Advent season, wherein I had pushed the church through a highly dramatic four-week liturgy that was crafted, organized, and directed entirely by me. Now it was January, and I was worn thin.

He told me of a phenomenon in high-functioning individuals. I don't remember the technical name, but the gist was that periods of heavy exertion are followed by a period of mental slump and recuperation. This struck me as true. I remembered such things from my theatre days in college. After the intense weeks of a production, there would be a day or two of complete crash—a melancholia, a sort of mourning the show's closing as of the death of a good friend. Sometimes I would even catch a cold, as if my immune system were coming down from a high as well.

He said that for younger people, this psychic recession might last only hours, or a day or two, but as we age the time it takes to go through it lengthens, up to a couple of weeks or longer.

All that rang true. I had just come through a large and extended "performance," and I was not bouncing back as quickly as the younger me was used to.

So he was right ... but he was also horribly wrong. He didn't know the long and uninterrupted season of labor had been not a mere four weeks of Advent but years ... the whole lost decade of my thirties as I pursued my doctoral degree to the exclusion of much else that made life worth having. I had forgotten the art of rest. I knew only how to work—to do good. And it was catching up with me.

Of course, I misunderstood his point. He probably meant something like *So go rest. You need it.* Instead, I heard the only thing my works-oriented mind would allow me to hear: *Don't worry. It'll pass.* So I kept working ... and I worked till the day I was shown the door.

Reflecting on things others said to me after the detonation, I apparently had hidden all this erosion pretty well. People expressed shock at "how suddenly" I fell apart. Yes, I'm sure it looked that way. From the outside, I appeared an effective classroom instructor and pulpiteer. My final sermon and lecture were as effective and potent as any that preceded them. And then I was gone—never saw the inside of a classroom or stood at the working end of my own pulpit again. In that way, yes, it was sudden.

But doesn't the blowout of public figures—politicians, celebrities, athletes—always look that way? It almost has to. While we concede that those on the stage or screen are *just like us*—one pant leg at a time sort of thing—we still fantasize about their private life in terms of their public one. If they're charismatic and successful in their public work, then they must have a beautiful private life as well, right?

Thanks to social media, this sort of deception is now available to all people. Any of us can present an online version of ourselves that has it all together while our private selves are sinking in depression, self-loathing, and despair. Those unwise enough to allow their private hells to show up on their feed get unfollowed. So we are incentivized to lie. For pastors and church workers, this was all true before the advent of social media … and in spades. Thus the downfall of a public figure will almost always *appear* sudden.

That's where I disagree with my psychological colleague. It's possible to be depressed and still show up for work. People do it all the time. It's possible to be very good at your job—potent, charismatic, and powerful—while being dead on the inside.

The key is motivation. If you're working at a job you dislike, then yes, a depressive episode will likely leave you bedridden and useless. If all you're doing is keeping up an online image, yes, a minor blue period may be all it takes to bring your budding blog to a halt. But what if one is motivated by something greater—something like religious fervor or parental obligation? What if people's lives depend on your keeping the mask on? How long will a truly broken soldier continue to man his post if he believes his comrades are counting on him for their survival?

You could not have a greater misunderstanding of God's goal than in the determination to destroy yourself "for the sake of others."

The dark truth is if enough terrible responsibility is laid on someone's shoulders, the consequences of their failure made sufficiently great and devastating to others, then a depressed person will *still* perform … for a time. They will continue like a machine till the whole system suddenly collapses. Never underestimate the temporary resilience of the despairing martyr.

This ever-increasing weight of responsibility coupled with the certain knowledge of coming shame made this the darkest and most horrible phase of the descent—to be dead, to know you're dead but knowing that if you let it show, you will destroy people. For nearly eight zombified months, I trudged on, preaching a sermon every Sunday—good sermons, sermons people loved, sermons that changed lives. What choice did I think I had?

How Shall We Then Live?
Know That Adamantine Machines Still Break

The machine that's allowed to run low on oil will not last, and its eventual failure will be more costly than regular maintenance would have been. This warning may be coming too late for you, but we would do well to remind ourselves that the church has only one Savior—and it isn't you or me. Only One was sufficient to lay down his life for the sake of others.

You are beloved and valuable but not indispensable.

God desires our participation, but does not *need* us—and certainly does not desire empty martyrdom on the terms your depressed soul is offering.

God desires your flourishing. Christ's work had that as its aim. You could not have a greater misunderstanding of God's goal than in the determination to destroy yourself "for the sake of others."

Never make the mistake of thinking you're doing fine because you're still checking off the boxes on your to-do list. Showing up for work is not the same as being spiritual or healthy or alive. Just because you're still moving at top speed doesn't mean you're not headed for a cliff.

CHAPTER 8

FACING DIVINE SILENCE

He drank. He drank to forget. He drank for the numbness it gave. And now even as it was killing him, he drank so the end would come sooner.

She held his hand as the darkness grew. His breath quickened. His strength failed. In one last despairing heave, he gasped, "How come you never told me you loved me?"

The reply was certain, calm, and quiet. "I did. I told you every day."

"Really? Well, I never heard you!"

"No, my love, you didn't."

S O WHERE WAS GOD IN THE FACE OF MY LOOMING DISASTER? Was I beyond the divine reach? Was there no salvation from the hell I had chosen? I suppose theologians of different stripes would give different answers. Some would say my situation was merely a metaphor for all people's true situation. We're *all* so lost that unless God reaches down and gives us special grace, we can do naught but wallow in the hell we've chosen. Other theologians would say God has indeed done all necessary to free us and that all that stands between us and that freedom is our unwillingness to choose it.

This is an age-old debate that seems important until you find yourself actually in a hell of your own making. Then it no longer seems to matter. All theologies lose their luster when you realize you've lost the power of choice and no sufficient grace is appearing. It is a cruel feature of the descent into hell that our ability to foresee our fate lasts longer than our power to change it.

In hindsight, I see that I did try to talk about it—inadequately, but the record is there. That summer I preached through the Minor Prophets—a book a week—a survey of all the little obscure books in the middle of the Bible. It was great fun. But I remember with particular horror the sermon on Habakkuk, as he stands the night watch on the wall of the city, staring out, wondering where God is in all this chaos. I saw this as a chance to be "authentic," so I shared a bit of my struggle with depression. Read between the lines of the transcript, and you will hear all the chapters of this book so far writing themselves large on the wall behind my pulpit as I preached.

You've all felt it … that moment where you realize some dreams just can't be had. Well, I began to wrestle with feelings of being cheated, manipulated, lied to. Having been told that if you "follow Jesus's way"—which really meant the view of Christianity that the Christian social engineers espoused— you'd be complete and fulfilled. And now having achieved everything they wanted me to achieve … I was neither.

This was an earthshattering realization, because it landed on me something like, *You didn't follow your dreams when you were young because the Jesus you were told about "didn't care about that," and now, even though you've realized the lie, if you're going to follow Jesus, you still can't.* So imagine feeling as though you had lost your past and future in one blow, right in the moment of reaching what you had always been told were the highest possible career goals. And worse, that it was Jesus himself who had stood in the way of you living out your authentic self.

The feeling that Jesus himself deceived and betrayed

you is a world-shattering feeling. The sudden suspicion—the doubt—that it's all a lie made up by the Christian social engineers to turn you into something useful. And every time someone would come up to me and say, "God is using you greatly" ... I realized I was beginning to hear, *God is using you.*

That, of course, drove me to do what any of you would do—fall to my knees. On my face in tears, night after night, unable to eat or sleep. *Why this? Why would you do this? Why now? Was I not being faithful with everything I had before?* Had I not given up enough stuff already to do this?

And do you know what God said? Nothing ... Crickets.

A week later I emailed my brother about that sermon.

I was reviewing my sermon [audio] last night. Denise was in the other room nursing Asher and listening. She came to me in tears afterward and said, "I can see it now, but I can't understand it. You're saying everything right; you're preaching the absolute truth, and yet God is not helping you. He's left you to suffer alone, and I don't know why or how it can end. Why isn't he helping you?" She is finally seeing it for what it actually feels like.

And yet I see what God is doing in the lives in this church through it ... It's impossible and amazing. I can't see the way forward. It's so dark. Does God really destroy one life so that many may live? He did so with Christ!

Is this diabolical or divine? Is it a form of oppression or a stigmata? Is it like Job—a pact between God and the Devil to destroy the faithful just to prove their faithfulness? Is it so that I am to be crucified so my flock may live, grow, and have life? Is this what it means to be like Christ? To suffer on behalf of others? That if I endure it, many shall be saved!? By MY stripes they shall be healed?

I know the answer is supposed to be NO, but this is like nothing I've ever experienced. It's no good telling me it's not God's way or will, that God doesn't do that—HE IS DOING IT!

The urge to rebel grows—then the pointlessness of a rebellion becomes clear. Where would I go? My whole life is locked now, without alternative or option. The choice to rebel is to lose all immediately, the choice to remain is to lose all slowly. I am no longer an agent of my own destiny.

God has left me alone at exactly the point where I most need aid and comfort. I can only conclude that this is one of the central questions at stake: How much isolation can this soul bear before it breaks?

I can't see the end of this. I'm stumbling blindly onward only because I know obedience demands it, but I don't know the destination or even why I should keep running except that my family starves if I don't.

Okay, I've talked myself into numbness. I can go back to writing my sermon for THIS Sunday. Thanks for listening.

P.S. A. W. Tozer said, "It is doubtful whether God can bless a man greatly till He has hurt him deeply." What a horrible truth if it is true.

Silence or Deafness?

Christians of every generation have written and reflected on the phenomenon of God's silence. The prophet Isaiah himself wrote, "You are a God who hides himself."[12] The sons of Korah wrote the darkest psalm in the canon: "You have taken from me friend and neighbor—darkness is my closest friend."[13] This dark journey is perhaps best known by St. John of the Cross's label, *the dark night of the soul.*

This isn't the same as depression. While it does threaten the soul with possible destruction, a true dark night is supposed to have a purging, faith-building effect. It's sent by God for divine purposes and dissipates at the divine timing. Those who have endured a true dark night will speak of it with both horror and reverent thanksgiving and will say it was one of the periods of greatest spiritual growth in their lives.

I was not enduring a dark night of the soul (though at the time, I called it that). I have already said some kinds of depression are self-inflicted, and I now believe divine silence can be too. The act of making yourself unable to hear the divine voice is *not* the same as the dark night. Yes, it will be dark and feel like night, but the comparison ends there. We must be careful attributing to God our own folly.

You may recall Uncle Andrew in C. S. Lewis's *The Magician's Nephew*, who, stranded in Narnia, finds the idea of talking animals so repellant to his modern sensibilities that he diligently works to convince himself that they're really only cawing, barking, baying, and bleating. With his typical pith, Lewis observes, "Now the trouble about trying to make yourself stupider than you really are is that you very often succeed."[14] When Aslan finally comes to ask what this old sinner would have him do, Andrew can hear nothing but growls. He cowers in fear. It was not the fault of the Lion but of the fool in his folly. Andrew's terrors are caused not by divine silence but by willful deafness.

How Shall We Then Live?
Silence as Invitation or Warning

The silence of God is not always an invitation to growth. Sometimes it's an invitation to repent. Under the effects of self-deception, obsession, and fear, we possess the power to cast the veil of the holy over even our greatest foolishness ... for a time.

> The deafening silence in which you walk may also be a last-ditch effort to rouse you from your callousness and folly.

If God seems silent and you feel abandoned, it may indeed be a true dark night. If so, rejoice in the darkness, for God is about to produce something in you that can only grow in darkness. But the deafening silence in which you walk may also be a last-ditch effort on God's part to rouse you from your callousness and folly. The two conditions may feel much the same, but they are not. One is a grace, the other a mercy—a final opportunity to be rescued from the end you've chosen. What sounds to you like growling may actually be the Lion whispering your name.

CHAPTER 9

Hearing the Bullet

A Final Plea

*The police officer leaned out the window of the office building,
begging the fellow on the ledge not to jump. The officer had
tried every argument he could think of, but the suicidal man
acted as if nothing really mattered.*

*He tried another angle. "But, sir, none of us know the future.
Things may be tough now, but they could always improve. If
you jump ... well, that's the end."*

*The man only shrugged and said, "Nah, I can always
change my mind halfway down."*

WHILE STRUGGLING THROUGH DEPRESSION, I CONTINUED
preaching a sermon every Sunday, because that was my
job. I think I kept my despair out of my sermons fairly well ...
whether or not I should have. I've mentioned how my treatment
of Habakkuk's dilemma became a sort of window into my struggle. Here's another fragment of that sermon.

If I am not to be the greatest of hypocrites, I am compelled despite great reluctance to tell you something of my
own journey over the last year and a half. I don't want to

because I know it will cost me. Somewhere in the back of the mind people want or even need the person who stands here to be above such things—even though publicly you would say, "He's just a guy like anyone else." It's not so. When you fail, you hurt a dozen people. If I fail, I hurt hundreds. And so there is the unstated pressure to manage perceptions, to give the image of strength … when the truth is I'm just trying to hold on …

Four months later I was unemployed and unemployable. And yes, you heard me right, I saw it coming. People often hear the bullet coming and yet seem unable to duck.

In the preceding chapters, I have outlined some distinct moments in the run-up to self-destruction. Other possible ones exist, of course. I know a pastor whose affair required hiding in the trunk of his lover's car to avoid discovery. Another used a camera to slyly film his obsessive target in compromising situations. Do not think that because your self-deceptions, fears, or regrets involve forbidden gold, forbidden status, or forbidden fruits that you can avoid the end. Sins will out themselves eventually. Like Frodo's ring, our obsessions long to return to their ultimate master and will betray us.

At this point you may well ask why I haven't spoken more on prevention. Why not try to help people *before* they self-destruct? The answer depends on who you are.

One obvious answer is that I have done nothing through this section *but* speak of prevention. If you're a student, pastor, or employee of a Christian organization, then by this point of the book you should have a pretty good sense of the shape of the sin lurking at your door. For you, this has all been a warning.

Perhaps you really mean *Why aren't you trying harder to dissuade the person in imminent peril of self-destruction? Why are you merely describing?* The short answer is this: Because of my own journey, I've come to believe that those with the acute self-induced fever of destruction cannot be *talked* out of it. There is no salvation for such a person ... till after the fall. The power to turn back was forfeited long ago by their own will. The alcoholic can no longer put down the bottle despite an earlier time when he could have. That time has passed.

Yet I do believe in a God who can, even now, work miracles. So I will, here at the close of Part 1, make a final attempt to reason with those who are in immediate peril of throwing it all away in some depressive, addictive, or obsessive episode—to those who are so far down that road they can already hear the bullet coming.

I watched my own life unravel in slow motion—ominously and with certainty. The suspense only made me more desperate.

Does this sound like you? The particulars of your story differ, I'm sure. But you already know the analog in your own life—that relationship you can't escape (or maybe the one you can't have), that choice you've made so often that it doesn't feel like a choice anymore, that itch you keep trying to scratch even though your soul is red and swollen from digging at it. You know what it is—the stolen funds, the photos taken or sent, the money paid, the files saved, the rendezvous kept. We both know you can't take any exit I could offer. You, too, hear the bullet coming but have lost the power to duck.

Because your case is that desperate, I'm going to risk saying the hardest things no one else will say to you. If the Holy Spirit should so use it to force you into the light, God be praised. But more likely I'm giving you something to come back to later when it has all come apart and you're looking for a way to interpret what has happened to you.

You Are Here

Let's start by rehearsing your real situation. By now, you must know you're lying to yourself. Whatever that thing you're clutching—the person, habit, possession, or value—part of you already knows it's killing you slowly. Yet you continue to clutch, telling yourself you can handle it, or that it will eventually work out, or that if some impossible change of circumstance were to happen, you could finally be happy or get the thing you want.

It's a lie.

I don't mean you don't believe the lie. I know you do. I was absolutely sure that everything I told myself and others was true. I was actually convinced the poisonous relationship killing me was a performance of Christian charity. Only now, years later, after the fever has broken, do I see it for the self-deception it was.

In the end, it doesn't matter if your particular hunger is for power or peace, a lost youth or a future legacy. If you're like I was, then like an addict, you will gorge your disordered longing till you feel justified in casting aside spouse, children, career, health, and even your own life in desperate and despairing bids for the unattainable.

But it is still a lie.

In truth, you are Cain holding the club, beckoning to Abel. Preparing for the moment that will change all possible futures for you. You are willingly putting yourself in the path of the bullet that will kill you.

A Final Invitation

Is there no solution, then?

Yes, of course there is. I've already said it. The answer to bloated raging desire has always been *contentment*. The chances are excellent that you still have some wonderful things and people in your orbit—that great beauty still exists in the life you now disdain. Others can see it. Perhaps they've tried to tell you, but you're blind to the color, deaf to the music. I don't fault you. Despair is like that. It takes and takes and leaves us deaf and blind and desperate—a tyrant you'd rather die with than live without.

But there's another possibility.

Perhaps the overwhelming grief you feel is not a threat but an invitation to let go. That ghastly thing in your hand is not a thing to be clutched but a seed to be sown.

Give it to the ground and let it die.

That's how you grow something beautiful out of something painful. Contentment is found in the release. Nothing worth having in life is gained by clutching. Most things are ultimately attained by giving them up, and that is what makes joy such a surprise when it comes.

But such an invitation to happiness will probably not be compelling to you. If not, it means you have chosen the way of fear. If you've lost your taste for the carrot, only the stick remains. Let me, then, share what is about to happen, so that when it does, you may then believe I knew what I was talking about.

It Is Even at the Door

No addiction, obsession, or depression can continue forever unchecked. It's only a matter of time before the bullet finds its mark. I can't predict what that tragedy will look like. I never could have foreseen the manner of my own downfall. God only knows—the loss of a marriage or friendship, the death, the loss of career or health or reputation or liberty. You might reply you've lost all those things already and yet the itch persists. All that means is you have not yet hit bottom, and worse is waiting.

I dare not pull punches here. All that you fear will happen if you continue down this path *will* happen. You are about to expose to the world what you've made yourself into in your despair. And I can assure you that all the things you fear people will say about you *will* be said—that's what people are like. So begin even now to make peace with that fact. Learning to live with crippling shame will be a central effort of life after this. Trust me, I know.

Feel free to lash out at me with enraged explanations of why this won't be *your* end, why you'll be the exception, how all this self-torture will somehow still result in happiness. I welcome your anger. It means you still have enough self-respect to care about what you're becoming. And you can't shock or hurt me whatever your reply. I'm too far down the road you're now walking to care what others think of me. I have to be. That's what life looks like on this side of the decisions you are now contemplating. I would spare you this if I could. Leave the fair, Pinocchio, before you become an ass. Your Geppettos, whoever they are in that life you now detest, may not be perfect, but they love you, and that is a better offer than you will get from Monstro when he comes.

How Shall We Then Live?

What, then, should you do when all this finally comes to pass? Mark this chapter so you can come back to it. You'll know when it's time. It means you're ready for the rest of this book.

That said, I do have one central piece of advice upon which all else depends. You're feeling as though you have nothing left? You've lost all that you had? You're perhaps even now realizing how good you had it and what a fool you were to trade it all for the desolation you're now feeling? Well, that's actually an improvement—the first step back to sanity is to be able to speak truth to yourself.

> The horrible destructive choice you're about to make—the thing that makes it all come crashing down—is not half so important or defining as the choices you will make after that.

Because, well, you *have* been a fool, and so was I. But here's what I've learned, and this is the single most important thing for you to remember.

The horrible destructive choice you're about to make—the thing that makes it all come crashing down—is not half so important or defining as the choices you will make after that.

Yes, you will still get to make choices. Of course, others will, too, in response. Let them; that's their right.

Once it all comes crashing down, the real choosing begins. You will either choose to give up—only to discover that what you thought was the bottom really wasn't (there is always a deeper level of hell you can descend into), or you will choose to change. You can embrace the fact you were a fool—as we've all been—and now that the fever has broken, you can begin the hard work of rebuilding your life on a firmer footing.

That is the goal of this book—to help you do that.

It won't be the same life you had. Resurrection is never about getting the old life back. It's about new things. It may feel like the bullet has killed you, but really, that's yet to be determined. You are no longer able to avoid the bullet; that choice is already made. But whether the wound is terminal has not yet been decided.

You have before you now a journey that will require several years of consistently making good choices before you really feel like you're coming out of it. Don't give up. Get a calendar, get a journal, get a hobby, get a counselor, friend, pastor, or spiritual director. Don't try to do this alone. Most of the pages of this book are still ahead. That alone should tell you that stories like ours don't end with the explosion … or they need not.

PART 2

SURVIVING THE EXPLOSION

Perspectives for When It All Comes Apart

There were things, your own acts,
from which you could never recover.
Something was killed in your breast:
burnt out, cauterized out.

—George Orwell, *1984*

CHAPTER 10

A WINDOW ON TRAGEDY

A young man was bemoaning with many tears his ill fortune to his father when a knock came at the door.

Looking out the window, the youth groaned, "Oh, no, it's your neighbor, Old Man Jones."

"Well, let him in, son. He's just the man for this. He's very wise."

"What could he possibly say that would make any of this better?"

"Not a thing. He won't even try. That's what makes him so wise."

So the explosion has happened. The thing you were dreading has come to pass. The marriage dead, the career ruined, the lies revealed, the arrest made. Your attempts to hide, evade, and manipulate the data have failed, and the story is now in the open at last. Or at least someone's version of it is—and probably not yours. The ramifications of your choices are only now making themselves clear, and perhaps they've taken your breath away with their vigor and scope.

Let me start by saying I am sorry.

Pain is still painful, sorrow still sorrowful, even when we've had a share in making it. In their rush to aid victims, people are usually pretty unsympathetic to the agony the perpetrator has brought on himself. This is perfectly understandable and even in a narrow sense correct, but it doesn't make your losses any easier to bear. Few things are more discouraging than being told your pain doesn't count.

In cases like ours, justice is almost always left to third parties. I hope that, even in the midst of your efforts to just keep breathing, you can see it must be this way. You're no better suited at this moment to determine justice than those on the other end of your story. It's a basic principle of suffering. It makes you an unreliable narrator even of your own life.

When I reached this stage of my story, I began to suspect that all the songs on the radio that said suffering makes you stronger were lying. Sometimes suffering doesn't make you stronger— sometimes it just kills you. This possibility left me jittery, frightened, and hardly able to hold on as the losses mounted. I imagine that you, now, are in a similar situation.

So I'm going to do you a kindness, if I can. In these next few chapters, I'm going to try to walk with you through this.

I know this feels like the end—and indeed it *is* the end of some things—but it's also the beginning of a longer journey, and how you traverse these next few steps will make a lot of difference to where you come out. It will be two to three years from this moment before you really begin to feel anything like yourself. So start prepping your mind now for that journey. And for God's sake, keep breathing. That's the first step to getting through this.

Someday, when all the dust has settled, you will say to yourself, *What's next?* And you'll discover life is still there, waiting to be lived. Life doesn't quit, so you mustn't either.

Keep breathing.

Your response in this phase of the journey will determine what Life 2.0 looks like. Let me say it again: The most defining choices you make are not the ones that got you here but the ones you are about to make. Every morning, you'll have to choose whether to give up or get up.

I've been there, and I'm here to tell you what it's like to get up every damn day … and live.

The Rest of the Story

For this to work, I'll have to tell you a bit more about my own little Chernobyl. This is the part of the narrative that's hardest to tell. Partly because it is sordid and shameful, but just as much because the details are difficult.

I, too, am unreliable here; I know it. In the spasms of crisis, the mind retains only certain things. Anyone who has endured a car accident or a violent trauma will tell you that some emotional details are razor sharp—sharper than you would ever want them to be. Others become muddled, as if the mind just failed to record properly. If you talked to Lorelai, I concede that her version of these events would look different. I am not saying her version is wrong. I simply don't know anymore. And I confess I'm even a little grateful for the fuzziness. It is a divine mercy, perhaps, that we don't have to carry the full burden of our folly around with us in high-definition memory. How could we live? It would turn a well-known adage on its head: Time wounds all heals.

The great risk is that the following will be seen as a mere attempt to reframe my story. I cannot deny that the urge exists. Having had my story framed so poorly by the media, I certainly have in me a desire to "set the record straight." It's a desire I must daily die to. In recent years I have constantly prayed that when the time came for me to put my story in print, I would have the grace to do so honestly and for the right reasons. You will have to be the judge.

Let's be clear, however, that I offer no defense for my actions. They were foolish and wrong. Good motives don't change that— if indeed they were good. My own motives are one of the things

I can hardly now recall. Thinking of these events now is like watching an old movie starring actors whose names you can't remember. For all legal and moral purposes, I must affirm that me, myself, and I alone did them. But in the subjective world of the mind, it is hard to recognize that sad, broken, Gollum-like creature as myself. That gives me a strange sort of emotional distance from the events, which I suppose is necessary to the telling. If I had to enter that warped soul-space again as I felt it then, surely I would be unable to say anything. So forgive the clinical distance. We tell our stories as we are able.

Men Love Darkness Rather Than Light

We had an agreement, Lorelai and I. Every attempt to save her house from foreclosure had failed. The money was gone—even many thousands of my own dollars I'd poured in to get the mortgage current. (Yes, obsession is costly in all sorts of ways.) All that was left to us was prayer. She had requested that the church elders spend some time at her house performing prayer walks around the property. To my knowledge, the elders had never done so, so I offered to do it myself, and I had done so on several occasions throughout the summer.

The fall night before the foreclosure deadline, I was teaching an evening class at the seminary, getting out around 9:00 or 10:00. As I drove home musing on her situation, I remembered she'd told me that morning she was going out with her new boyfriend and that her kids were all at her mother's for the night.

Here enters the great folly born of months of frustrated self-deception. I realized this was my last chance for a final prayer walk around the property before the bank foreclosed. Arriving, I began my walk around the house, only to discover that, on the back side of the house, lights were on in one room and shadowed blurs moved across the window. The house was a split-level, and this window was halfway between a ground floor and a second-story window. In a perfectly ridiculous coincidence Murphy himself could not have orchestrated, a stepladder was propped against that side of the house near the window. I had been in the house several times and so knew this window was in Lorelai's bedroom.

Here my recall of motives abandons me. Some combination of concern, curiosity, and lechery drew me to the window. No one was supposed to be home, yet the bedroom lights were on. Reason failed. Folly ruled. Using the stepladder, I looked in the window. As Murphy would have it, Lorelai and her boyfriend had not gone out (or had come back early) and decided to engage in … intimate congress.

A dozen seconds of shocked observation reduced me to an internal mess. I leapt down and ran for my car, tears beginning to flow. I had just received the blow that would crack ten months of self-deception. I saw in that moment, in a way I could deny no longer, what I had become, what I had turned myself into. In my privation, I'd debased myself to the level of a peeping tom.

I drove to the church, where I sat in the parking lot, bellowing and crying over my folly and lost integrity. I knew now—could no longer deny—that everything for which I'd worked for twenty years was about to go away. I knew the charade was killing me, and I knew I didn't care. I knew I had to speak. Come what may, it was the only way out.

I went home and slept on the couch. Denise was already in bed, and I was too miserable to join her. In my church office the following morning when the YOO-HOO! came, I trudged down, coffee mug in hand, preparing my career-ending *mea culpa*. We sat, and I tried, with many hesitations and pauses, to launch into my confession. Then the children's pastor wandered in looking for sticky notes or something, and I lost my nerve.

Here I abbreviate the rest of that tortured day to come to the point. That evening Lorelai texted me and asked if I wanted to go out for drinks with her and her beau, something she'd never done before. So perhaps, paranoia whispered, by some mystery I couldn't fathom they knew and wanted to confront me. It spooked me, and I declined, but after some hard thinking, I decided again that I couldn't live like this anymore. So I went to her house and met her boyfriend standing in the yard (I don't know why he was standing there). We went inside, and I confessed to them both. Their shock and anger were legitimate and justified. I left her house, went home, and laid it all out for my wife. Then I wrote emails telling the lead pastor I had to speak with him in the morning.

That might have been the end. Horrible, yes. I would have left the church, and the blast radius would have been roughly the footprint of the church property.

What I didn't know was that, having seen movement in the window on the previous night, Lorelai and her boyfriend had filed a police report. When the detective returned a few days later to follow up, they told him they now knew who it was. The detective then came to my door, and I confirmed the whole story. When all was said and done, the two of them decided they wanted to exercise their legal right to press the charges.

In the coming weeks, as my lawyer and the prosecutor dickered over whether what I'd done was a felony or a misdemeanor and whether there should be one count or two, Denise and I languished. I resigned from the church, but since the seminary knew nothing of it, I continued teaching, hoping unreasonably that I would be able to salvage one of my careers.

Sadly, at one of the hearings, a local reporter happened to be present and splashed the story of the "Peeping Pastor" all over Michigan. As it spun from station to station, website to website, the eventual version had me driving around local neighborhoods with an extension ladder in my pickup, filming random couples having sex. Then the crank calls, threats, and other inconveniences began. But I get ahead of myself. The following chapters will discuss these things in their proper place.

Everything that follows, however, is grounded in experience. I don't know if that makes me an expert or a fool—probably both—but if you will let me walk with you through this crisis, then neither of us will have to face our folly alone.

THE BLESSING
OF DISCOVERY

"Grandpa, Grandpa, come here! What's that?"

The old woodsman lumbered up to where the little boy peered down into the sprung bear trap. He stroked his stubbly chin. "Don't see that too often now. Looks like the fore leg of a gray fox."

"But where's the rest of it?"

"He probably chewed off his own leg and bolted off that-away." He pointed a gnarled finger at drops of blood leading off into the woods.

The boy was aghast. "That's horrible. Why would he do that?"

"Well, if the choice was between dying in the trap with four legs or getting out of it with only three, which would you choose?"

WHEN EVERYTHING BLEW UP, HERE'S WHAT I DIDN'T expect. I did not expect to feel utter calm. But I did. People commented on it. In the weeks between my resignation from the church and the newspapers getting hold of the story, I continued teaching at the seminary. In that time, no less than three students said to me something like, "Professor, you look different." One who'd known me a long time even said, "You're looking more like your old self." Apparently, my ten-month self-inflicted incarceration with Lorelai had left marks—stains—that even now, mere days and weeks later, were already starting to rinse off. I had no idea my condition had been so visible to others. I thought I had hidden better than that.

Even Denise began to talk about "having me back," and even more I was shocked to find myself welcoming the attention. I actually wanted to be back. Already I was beginning to see what a remarkable person Denise had been through it. After all, she was still there.

Again, not after years of therapy. No, almost immediately— within hours and days, once I was no longer walking into the church office every day or getting texts—my spine began to straighten. I remember looking in the mirror as I got out of the shower and thinking for the first time, *Wow, I have lost weight. It doesn't look very good either.* I found myself eating again. I cannot express how quickly and radically my outlook on life changed— started to revert to older default settings. I began to feel things I hadn't felt in a really long time—gratitude, contentment.

Even when the police detective came to the door, I poured out the whole story with more ease than I'd said anything in almost a year. Upon hearing my tale of woe, he looked at me sympathetically as he clicked off his Dictaphone and said, "Well, these things happen for a reason," which I thought a remarkable mercy on his part. I wish I knew his name so I could thank him personally.

Three days later, he came and got me, and I was fine with that. He was gentle, counseling me on what to wear and letting me change my clothes and say goodbye to Denise. He even waited till we'd left the house before he put the cuffs on so Denise wouldn't have to watch. Even then, I was shocked that I felt no anxiety. Even as I sat in the holding cell at the police station not knowing whether I would go home that night or go upstairs in green scrubs to eat Spam on a shingle—clowns to the left of me, jokers to the right—I could not help smiling and thinking, *Well, nothing bad has actually happened to you yet.*

Denise did bring me home that night, so I didn't have to go upstairs. Bad things can happen upstairs, and that might have changed the trajectory of this story significantly. But for all the threat of it, I felt only a deep calm.

In the coming days, when the media trucks pulled into our driveway, I stood at the door and thanked the reporters for coming with a perfect serenity. When the FOX 17 truck got stuck sideways in the driveway on the early-December ice, I even walked down the hill and offered them coffee as they waited for the tow truck. We talked for ten minutes about Michigan winters before they got over their chagrin enough to ask me if I had any comment.

I didn't.

Over the coming weeks I chatted freely with the crank callers who posed as former students of mine trying to get me to admit things on the phone till they got tired and hung up. I read the comments about me following the online news stories, comments based on no or bad information—"Professor of Shagmatic Theology"—and laughed at the infinite scope of human cleverness.

Family and friends continued to comment on how well I seemed to be standing up to it all. And I was shocked to hear them say it. Truly shocked. Because this felt like about the easiest thing I'd done in the past year.

How was this possible? As Rome burned around me, how could I stand there calmly playing my fiddle? From whence came all this peace?

Unexpected Deliverance

I wish I could say this quietude of mind was a result of my deep faith in God, my belief in divine care, love, or superintendence. But I'd be lying. I was actually pretty sore at God, pissed with the seminary, angry at the church. I'll get to all that later, but it would be simple lying to say it was "my faith" that gave me peace.

It wasn't.

Its source was far simpler and animalian—I was free. The mounting losses were a small price to be free from the hell of the previous ten months. That I would never again be summoned by the YOO-HOO!. That I would never have to endure the inner war of wanting to get deeper in while also wanting to get out. That I wouldn't have to drive out in front of an eighteen-wheeler. That I no longer had to lie to Denise or to myself.

Put that on the scales against unemployment, career loss, public shaming, and a looming criminal record—Oh my friend, there's no comparison.

Sméagol was free!

I could hardly understand, much less articulate, how color could so rapidly flood back into my world. Depression disappeared. I threw my antidepressants into the trash. I terminated my therapy sessions. I didn't need to "talk about it" anymore. It was done.

I knew what lay behind me, and so long as I didn't have to go back there, I knew I could endure anything. Who would have thought that in the face of the loss of everything, I would find contentment in just recognizing the face in the mirror as my own?

How Shall We Then Live? It's Only a Stage

Are you experiencing any sense of liberation, even amid the losses? If so, accept it as a gift. I'm sorry to say any sense of relief you're feeling is probably temporary—not out of some additional fault in you, but rather because your situation right now is fluid and overly dependent on other people's choices. Others are only now beginning to react to your implosion, and their response is about to wreak havoc on your mood.

Brace yourself.

Based on how some responded to it, I wonder if what happened in me is unusual. Some disbelieved it. At the same time students were telling me I looked more like myself than I had in a long time, some of our closest friends were still counseling Denise to leave me or throw me out. The elders at the church were taking all this renewed joy as a sign of impenitence. The justice system was trying to determine whether I was a threat to the community. Surely I had to be faking. Nobody turns around that fast. Was I just shamming, trying to limit the consequences of my choices? As Lorelai's boyfriend put it in a press interview, "He's not sorry he did it, only sorry he got caught."

> Any sense of relief you are feeling is probably temporary. Brace yourself.

This was the first indicator of the painful horizons that lay ahead. This sense of liberty wasn't to last. Many steps involving bitterness, anger, remorse, and shame awaited me, but in the earliest days of the scandal, I simply enjoyed being with my family and getting to know myself again. Oh, yes, bad days were yet to come. But for the first time in nearly a year I would be able to face them as myself—and oh, what a relief that was! Thank God, my life fell apart.

CHAPTER 12

Enter the Google

When Your Public Reputation
Gets Shredded

The priest of a small highland parish had lived an austere and abstemious life. He fasted twice a week and seldom ate meat. For more than four decades he had been a model of restraint to his congregation and was regarded as a man of stoic and upright character. Then one night in pursuit of an errant member of his flock, he found himself in the local pub.

"Aw, Father, have a drink with me," slurred the prodigal.

"No, my son, you must come with me. Your wife and children are—"

"Tell you what, Father. Have one wee drink with me, and I'll come along peaceful as a lamb."

So against his better judgment, the priest yielded and received his pint ... and then another. Unaccustomed to such spirits, the priest concluded the evening dancing on a table with his congregant, singing a bawdy tune.

As the two men nursed their aching heads the next morning, the rake said, "Now, Father, I hope you're not regretting our wee bit of fun. No harm done. We need never speak of it again."

The priest groaned. "I could live with the indiscretion, if only the town crier would shut up about it."

Y OU GET TO PICK YOUR CHOICES. YOU DON'T GET TO PICK your consequences. They will be what they will be, and no amount of raging, grieving, or bartering will change them. When my story went public in the most depressing ways, I was shocked by the surreal directions of the fallout. Suddenly strangers I met on the street thought they knew more about me than I did. And the hardest part was suspecting that all the horrid things they said about me might actually be true in some way I couldn't see.

A month later I showed up for my appointment at the barbershop where I'd been getting my hair cut for several years, except this time Judy met me at the door. "I'm sorry. I can't cut your hair."

I stood on the sidewalk with one eyebrow cocked.

"The management knows what you did, and they won't let any of the girls here cut your hair anymore."

To this day I don't know if that was the truth or if she just didn't want to cut my hair anymore and made up the story as cover. I don't blame her either way—the things the media said were as horrible as they were distorted. But that's the point. If you've made a choice that has blown up your life and public reputation, then what accompanies that is a loss of control over your own story. You are no longer in a position to dictate what people think of you.

A moment's reflection will make clear this was always the case. We *never* have any real control over what people think of us. As Jacque Abbadie reminded us, it's either *some of the people* or *some of the time* but never both. No amount of suave, carefully managed PR, or selective social media splashing can defend your reputation against a single negative word from a source people trust more. And it seems nobody has any control over Google searches.

The only real change here is that your situation has become unavoidably clear to *you*. Anything that makes us more aware of our real circumstances is always in the end a friend, but what is ultimately for our good seldom *feels* good. Eating less sugar is ultimately for our good, but it's certainly less pleasurable than a dish of ice cream.

The real question is not how I rehabilitate my public image but what place will my public image have in the new person I must now become. How important will others' opinion of me be? My guess is that reputation will now have to play a much smaller role than it has heretofore. This may be one of those pieces of luggage you must leave behind. And the reason is a very simple one.

If you make restoring your public image the thing you aim at, you will cut corners to get there, and while you may fool some of the people some of the time, you won't really be the person you're trying to present. You will only be a marketed representation of a fictitious self.

If, on the other hand, you allow concern over your public image to die, you will then be in a position to look deep within and actually change tiny bits of your soul. You have the opportunity to not *appear* different but to actually *become* different. I admit this is the harder journey. It takes longer, and the outcome is much less predictable.

If you attempt it, you will discover that you're suddenly open to being changed in directions you did not anticipate and may not like. Things about yourself you didn't know were even deficient will suddenly find themselves in the crosshairs. God, family, friends—even your enemies—will become a source of information about your core person. You will no longer be able to glide over small faults in your efforts to hide your great ones.

Don't misunderstand. This new person you will become is not a repudiation of the person you were. I still like the person I was before my trouble. In some ways I liked him better. He was more conscientious, more dedicated, more visionary, and had more energy and drive. In so many ways he was a more interesting person than the one I've become. But he was also very troubled. He was consumed with his image, destiny, and legacy. He spent far too much of his energy being afraid.

How Shall We Then Live? Digging Down

A few summers back, the county tore up the main road at the end of our street. They ripped off the blacktop, and instead of just laying down new asphalt and fixing the thing that was bothering us—a cracked-up road—they dug down a dozen feet with backhoes and made a royal mess of the whole highway.

Civil engineers apparently know things we, mere drivers, do not. Just putting down new blacktop would not have fixed what was really wrong—the fact that storm water had no place to go. So they engaged in the messier, deeper, more time-consuming labor of digging down and replacing the old and cracked drainage tiles. This is much less attractive work than just laying new road, and no driver would ever think to demand it. But it is the more important work, and it can be done only while the road is torn up.

You and I are the same way—we couldn't reach the deep things that needed fixing till the surface concerns had been torn away—painfully. Having your image publicly shredded is horrible, and no one would choose it, but it has now presented you with an opportunity. Are you going to just lay new road over the old one, or are you going to take the opportunity, when the road is already torn up, to dig down and fix the deeper issues? You may never get another chance to dredge so deeply, and you'll never be more aware of the need than now.

Just because your friends have disappeared, your career has dried up, and your stylist won't cut your hair, it's not the end. It's the beginning. Time for a counselor, life coach, or spiritual director. Time to do some digging. There's always another career, friend, or hair stylist but only one you. Start putting the effort where it's most needed, and those other, more visible issues will come right later.

> You may never get another chance to dredge so deeply, and you'll never be more aware of the need than now.

And if you're wondering whether I was ever able to get my hair cut—yes, I was. I booked an appointment under my pen name—Gordon Greenhill—at another location of the same company and ended up with Becky, who's been cutting my hair ever since and doesn't care about my backstory. Incidentally, she's far better than Judy ever was. So keep that in mind. Maintaining a good public reputation may be hard, but finding a good reliable haircut … well, that's nearly impossible. I suppose the lesson is this: Small blessings can grow on the back of big hairy tragedies.

CHAPTER 13

IT HURTS WORSE
WHEN CHURCHES DO IT

The kids shouldn't have been playing with the kitchen knives. They knew better.

The ER doctor examined the gashed arm gingerly. "Now, that doesn't look too bad. We'll have to clean it up a bit before I can suture." He called for a tray, and as he picked up the scalpel, the child screamed.

"Don't worry, sonny. I'm a doctor."

The fearful child cried, "That makes it worse! You ought to know better!"

WHEN THE PRESS BROKE MY STORY, THE SEMINARY PUT ME on administrative leave while my situation was "reviewed." To this day I don't know what that review consisted of, because that's one way businesses limit their liability. After several weeks of silence, I made a proactive appointment with Human Resources to ask questions about the process. When I arrived, I found the HR director sitting with the university's attorney. The meeting *opened* with me being told my contract was not being renewed, and a severance package would be extended so long as I signed an agreement forbidding me from speaking badly about the university. I was further told *they* would pack up my personal belongings, including the three thousand books in my office, and have a moving company deliver them to my door. I was not permitted in the building or to have any contact with students or colleagues while the process wound down. When a snowstorm prevented the office cleanout, I was allowed back into the seminary building on a deserted weekend to finish packing under the watchful eye of a security guard, who searched me at the end to ensure I wasn't stealing office supplies.

I declined the severance package, so I suppose I'm free to say anything I want. But the point here is that while I had expected my poor choices would ultimately cost me my position, I had not anticipated that the process would be so sterile and dehumanizing, particularly in an institution whose most publicly stated value was something like "Christlike in all we do." It felt like a colossal betrayal, not of me but of an institutional mission I'd spent fifteen years advocating in the classroom. This was my intellectual home. And it felt less like being released from a contract and more like being disowned by my family.

General Motors would have done the same thing in this position, and it would still have hurt, but I would have shrugged and thought, *Oh well, corporations are like that.* But when churches or religious institutions "forcibly deplane" someone, it feels like a betrayal and a violation of their faith commitments. Why is this? Why does termination from a church feel so different, even when it was mostly your own fault?

After spending several years thinking about this, I think I have an answer—*an* answer. There may be others, but this one has helped me make some peace with what happened, and I suppose that's the most you should expect from any answer. If you likewise have been "shown the exit ramp" from a church or parachurch organization, then I hope it will at least help you process your feelings.

The Church as Incarnational Business

Let's begin by noting some ways churches are *like* businesses. Whether you want to admit it or not, churches have many aspects of the business world baked into them by our society. You might say this shouldn't be so, but it is nevertheless a cultural reality. I was part of a home church of twenty people for over a decade, and despite our commitments to organic spiritual structures, we still had to file incorporation papers with the state and have by-laws with identifiable officers. There is no such thing as an abstract church—only churches incarnate within particular cultures, functioning within the confines of that culture. The American church lives in a particularly bureaucratic nation-state, and so long as tax codes, human resource requirements, and liability laws exist, the American church will have to interact with them.

And what's more, as churches grow in size and complexity, this administrative component grows proportionally. If churches are not going to divide into smaller communities, which I confess is where my sympathies lie, they will only survive by adopting more efficient processes. Now, if you wanted medical advice, you'd go to a doctor. Legal advice, to a lawyer. If the church needs help being efficient, where would you expect them to look but the world of business—that's where you find the efficiency experts.

But here's the rub. For all the ways the church is like Microsoft or Amazon—*must* be like Microsoft or Amazon—she is not Microsoft or Amazon. The church is not at its core a business, seeking to sell a product or make a profit. The church is entrusted with a responsibility with which no business in the world was ever entrusted. She is charged with caring for the souls of people, their spiritual well-being, their wholeness as creatures beloved by God. Likewise, Christian institutions such as universities, mission organizations, and soup kitchens participate in this mission in their own specialized ways as extensions of the church.

Thus, people rightly expect the church's primary interest to be the well-being of souls.

So whenever a church acts out of the business side of its identity in a way that causes pain to someone, that act will very naturally be perceived as an abandonment of the church's primary mission. It is predictable, inevitable, unavoidable.

Even when the church has done all she can to mitigate the most dehumanizing and soul-killing parts (which she *must* do), the fact remains that the pastor is now unemployed, the missionary has been sent home. Though every grace has been extended, the staff member is no longer there. After every best practice has been followed, the departing person can't help but feel as if their mother has thrown them out on the street to make their solitary way in the wide, wide world. And all these feelings of betrayal and abandonment will, in a sense, be justified. Justified because the church's primary mission is to heal, and it has instead done harm. Harm it could not help, perhaps, but harm nonetheless.

This is not a fiction, a merely emotional response, or a technicality. It really truly is much worse when a church terminates an employee. When it ceases to be scandalous, it means the church has ceased to be the church. The very sense of scandal alerts us to the differences at work in her. That feeling of betrayal is a signal, an invitation to consider the way of the church in the world.

How Shall We Then Live?
The Way of the Bureaucratic Church

How should we think about all this necessary harm? Of course, the answers change depending on who you are. Are you the one who was hurt by it, or are you one of those whose responsibility it is to inflict the hurt? Were this a book written to the pastors and administrators who have the terrible job of removing an employee for "moral turpitude" (or for any other reason), I would have very different things to say. But it is not. These reflections are aimed at people like you and me—the ones who are angry with the church because we were shoved out the window.

I've told you how your anger may be justified, but you should also understand how it might be unreasonable. I know speaking *rationally* to rage is a waste of time, but the sooner you're able to bring *reason* to bear upon your anger, the sooner you'll be able to leave the anger square of the board for a new one. If these thoughts are not compelling to you, no worries. That does not make them false. It may simply mean that you're not ready for them. Skip this chapter and come back to it later. Always give yourself the time you need.

First, your rage over the basic fact that your church *has* a business component is probably misplaced. You cannot realistically expect your church to unmoor itself entirely from its culture. You cannot ask or expect your church not to develop the business side of her identity. You should expect her to act justly, yes, but so long as your church is a thing that hires employees, she will be a thing that must terminate them. It is a logical necessity. The vision of a church without employees is a noble one, but that resolves one set of struggles by introducing a new set. A church without employees is, by definition, a church of volunteers. And anyone who's ever led volunteers knows this is no peaceable kingdom. It's only a different collection of problems.

Second, your accusations that your church or Christian ministry betrayed their values by removing you as they did are probably too simple. Yes, churches and parachurches are often ignorant of their actual values, but none of us should be surprised to discover that whatever core values or mission they espouse—Christ, the Kingdom, Universal Love, Compassion, whatever—alongside these magnanimous values lies a darker but equally compelling one—a value they will act from and not even know it—the value of *survival*. Pulitzer-winning playwright David Mamet once wrote, "It is the artist's job to create. It is the institution's job to continue."[15] Continuance and risk mitigation are the base pairs of institutional DNA.

Institutions fight for their survival with the primal ferocity of living things, and in itself this is a virtue. Institutions have a responsibility to their employees, their stated mission, and the constituency they serve. So when the institution meets a threat to its mission or existence, it acts instinctively to mitigate the risk. You must at least recognize that, in your case, your choices made you the risk.

It is true that when religious institutions forget or fail to *acknowledge* how deeply held that survival instinct is, their actions become uninterpretable to those who watch them. "How can Christ, Kingdom, or Love be the real central value when they go and do that?" This lack of candor breeds fear, suspicion, and cynicism.

But the point you would do well to remember is that for a church, university, or mission agency to act on its survival instinct is seldom personal and seldom preventable, like the reflexive jump when the hammer hits the knee. Most parts of this process had nothing to do with you personally. You might as well ask your antibodies not to fight the contaminant on the grounds that you ingested it on purpose. You have the right to grieve. But in your grieving, do not cling to the conclusion that the institution therefore cares nothing for people, the gospel, or its stated mission. That's just too simple. The church is trying to be both a soul-care organism and an organization with employees. There is no perfect walking of such a line. Mistakes will be made, and even when they are not made, harm will still be done.

Third, as you contemplate whether you ever wish to work in a ministry setting again, begin even now to reframe your understanding of such organizations. Nobody working at a church or parachurch organization should be under any illusion regarding the institutional aspects of their employer. Never idolize an institution. It is not so holy as to do no wrong, nor so wise as to do no harm. And by definition, it has no soul. Be a realist about what the church must be in an employment-driven culture such as ours.

Finally and most urgently right now, give yourself time before you respond publicly. Resist the urge to strike out. I don't mean that if you feel you've been legally mistreated, you shouldn't seek counsel. By all means, do so. I mean don't go making an ass of yourself on Facebook or Twitter. You will only end up hurting yourself worse if you create a vitriolic social media trail. I assume you want to get another job someday somewhere, and a social media record of your caustic temper tantrum—no matter how justified—will not help you land your next position. Instead, breathe deeply and take a long walk—especially if the reason you're not there anymore is your own fault. Even fools can be thought wise so long as they keep their mouths shut. A day may come when you can write your open letter, blog, or advice column from a position of having learned something that will be valuable to others. Who knows, maybe you'll even write a book about it.

> Give yourself time before you respond publicly. Resist the urge to strike out.

CHAPTER 14

ALL THOSE
FORBIDDEN FEELINGS

The accused sat in the dock, looking miserable. He hadn't meant to hurt anyone. He'd known he was too drunk to drive, but he was only a few miles from home. What could possibly go wrong?

The dead child's father was giving a tearful litany of his son's short life.

Overwhelmed, the accused burst into tears and put his head in his hands.

A woman in the gallery leaned over and whispered to her husband. "Look at him. He feels so wretched about it."

The man crossed his arms and harrumphed. "Who cares what he feels? He's the criminal."

THE ELDER MEETING TOOK PLACE TWO DAYS AFTER THE window incident. I had just finished a long, disjointed rant about how, for what it was worth, I could demonstrate from text and emails the consensual nature of the relationship, which was apparently something Lorelai had denied. I could likewise provide the names of several other men in her past whom she'd treated similarly. An awkward silence hung thick in the room as

I stumbled to a conclusion. Eventually, the head elder sighed. "Well, I guess our first order of business is to figure out how to tell the seminary all this."

The seminary would, of course, learn "all this" in a few weeks when the newspapers broke the story, but in that moment the only thought my muddled mind could grab onto was why one employer felt it appropriate to inform another about the details of my private life. I realize that, from the perspective of "the kingdom," it made a kind of sense for a church to inform a seminary of moral turpitude in one of its faculty. I get that. But at the moment, it struck me as wooly for your church to contact your employer with the intention of getting you fired. Further, it struck me as putting the church in extreme legal jeopardy regarding privacy.

So I burbled something like, "What? You can't do that. That's not even legal."

The head elder looked at me stonily. "Are you threatening us?"

That was the moment I knew everything was lost. I already knew my job at the church was over, but now I realized I would not even be believed, no matter how true my words. I had broken their trust so badly that even a cry of lament was heard as a threat of legal action.

It was my first glimpse of a terrible principle I would come to understand all too well. You will too. The principle is that you will not be allowed to say what you really feel. The guilty must hide their real feelings because people are willing to hear only one thing from them—"It's all my fault. I'm sorry."

The One Permissible Emotion

Right now, abject contrition is the only emotion you can express that will be received by others. You can tearfully repent and accept full responsibility for the situation. That is all. (Note: This is especially true if the criminal justice system is involved. If that's your story, please, see the appendix.)

Don't misunderstand me. You may actually feel sorry. You may have actually reached the conclusion that you *have* been a fool, that you *are* fully responsible for the situation—or at least your part of it. If that's the square you're standing in, then go with it. Be honest to that, and things will go a little less badly for you. This is probably the best-case scenario—when your emotional state matches the expectations of your friends, colleagues, family, or employer.

My experience, however, is that this is not likely. It's much more probable that you're a chaotic soup of emotions, of which remorse is merely one and perhaps not yet the dominant one. If you had a partner in crime who is denying their part or looks as though they will escape their share of responsibility, then you're probably also feeling defensive, angry, and bitter. If you're losing your livelihood, you're probably feeling fear and anxiety. If you're losing your marriage, your kids, your home, or your reputation, you're probably also feeling confused, ashamed, and lost. You may, as I did, even be feeling a mix of oddly pleasant emotions like relief or joy because you're no longer hiding, lying, or trapped. You may sit for long periods of time and simply shake as if with cold because your body just doesn't know what else to do. You may find you don't know how to answer the question, "How are you?" because it's so complicated and variable, changing minute by minute.

It is completely unreasonable to expect a person enduring such tidal forces to just be "sorry," as if that were a single and perpetual emotional state. Yet it is what people expect. You are the perp. You are the one who did the bad thing. "What right does he have to feel upset?"

Everyone is watching you—even people you haven't met— looking for signs of a repentance matching *their* profile of what repentance ought to look like. I think such people are naïve and wrong. But I'm not talking to them. I'm talking to you, and I don't want you to be as surprised by this phenomenon as I was.

As I've mentioned, within a week of everything exploding, I was actually feeling pretty good. I was free from the trap, the depression was ebbing, my marriage was on the mend. I could taste food again. I wanted others to know it, too, partly because I thought they understood the horrible things I'd endured over the last ten months.

They didn't.

I wrote what I took to be an uplifting email and sent it to the lead pastor with the instructions that when the time was right, he should share it with the church staff.

He shared it at the next staff meeting (a meeting Lorelai still attended). It said in part …

> It would be easy to just count the losses—my role at the church, the coming media attention that will cost me my seminary position and any future employment in my field, and will probably even kill my book deal. But I do not mourn; rather, please, rejoice with me! Denise and I have been enduring the greatest struggles of our marriage over the last two years almost to the point of separation, but the force of these events has caused us to rediscover one another. We have been reconciled and look hopefully on our family's future. My depression has broken and I feel more like myself than I have in years—as if great weights have been lifted. And most importantly God and I have found each other again, and that reunion is the sweetest of all. It feels absurd to say it, but in the moment where I have lost everything, I have been given back all that really matters. God is good, faithful, and kind. So stay strong, keep your eyes on the ball, serve the body, feed the sheep. I'll be cheering you on from the back row!

It was reported to me that when the note was read, the youth pastor crossed her arms and offered a biting, "Well, goodie for him! What about the rest of us?"

There's a lot to learn from this snippet—first perhaps is, don't write such emails. Nobody was interested in rejoicing with me because they were still on the event horizon of the black hole I'd created. They didn't want to hear or couldn't believe I was improving, and I can't blame them. As delivered, that email was profoundly tone-deaf and insensitive and may have even been a factor in the hard line the complainants took in the courtroom.

Right now the people in your life are so shocked or hurt or muddled that they're completely consumed with their own grief. It hasn't even occurred to them that you may be hurting too. And if they have thought of it, they probably resent it. You are the source of their grief. What right, then, do you have to be grieving also? This is how people think, and it is not absurd. It is very human.

> Begin to lean into the fact that nobody is interested in any emotion you feel right now except remorse.

What the church staff needed from me was a clear and concise declaration of my guilt and my owning of the pain they were enduring. If I were going to write an email at that time, I should've said *that*. I couldn't write such an email due to my legal situation, but that is really the only helpful thing I could've written. So the lesson is this: Begin to lean into the fact that nobody is interested in any emotion you feel right now except remorse. Nothing else will do you any good. If you understand that, it will perhaps help you not make the situation worse.

Explaining the Phenomenon

The cause of this myopia surrounding the perp's feelings is pretty straightforward. Most people's default sympathies are going to be with the victims—with the people hurt rather than with the perpetrator of the hurt. We are never more outraged than when we're empathizing with a wounded person. That's how people work, and you can make a strong case that they're right in so working.

But when a public figure betrays a group, a curious conflation of victim and outraged empathizer occurs. All the friends, family, coworkers, and congregants find themselves in both roles—that of victims with their own pain *and* that of observers, outraged by the pain of all the other victims. This convergence of victim and outraged observer creates an emotional soup in them as well. It justifies both their grief and their outrage and amplifies both in a feedback loop. There is just no bandwidth left in them to even consider *your* pain—after all, you're the cause of it all.

If you're anything other than remorseful in this early stage of the trauma, if you try to communicate your own anger or fear or relief, you will *appear* to be dismissing their pain. As if saying, "My pain is more important than yours." Can you think of anything more likely to increase the intensity of the feedback loop? You can hear it in the youth pastor's words, "Well, goodie for him! What about the rest of us?"

I know you hurt. I know your losses are great and may even become greater than your victims' (it is possible), but if you desire to not make your situation worse, know this: You cannot make this about you. It may feel unfair, yes, but it's also a natural consequence of the choices you made. If you want to survive, I encourage you to keep your own sense of outrage, anger, or fear close to the vest for now.

How Shall We Then Live?
Embittering Silence and the Judgments That Follow

Such a stuffing of emotion cannot help but embitter. I know. And I also know the last thing you need is another emotion to feel—bitterness. This is why I've spoken so frequently about the various squares on the game board. I've been trying to give you permission to stand in whatever square you're actually in. Bitterness may be the warranted response to the world's inability to consider your pain and loss. It may be completely normal to feel it. But even as you feel it, you must also recognize that bitterness is not a place you can live for long. It is only a square to pass through.

And you *will* pass through it. You will be stronger and understand yourself better *for* having passed through it. Times and situations will present themselves in the future for you to communicate those other emotions, perhaps even to the very people to whom you cannot disclose them now. And you may find that your time spent wrestling with these things in private will have actually prepared you to talk about them publicly later. If you doubt this, then I remind you that you're reading a book by exactly such a person doing exactly that thing you at present must *not* do.

When I speak of stuffing emotions, however, I don't mean it absolutely. The importance of a good therapist or spiritual director or, barring that, a close and sympathetic friend, cannot be overstated. You will need a place where you can safely vent your frustrations and other "unacceptable" feelings, but choose that location wisely.

A Final Admonition from Jesus

Try not to think badly of all these people who dismiss your losses as your just desert. I say *try* because you may be able to do so only as an abstract mental effort. Your emotions may refuse to cooperate. That doesn't make the mental effort meaningless. The effort not to hate is always a transforming effort.

Try not to judge harshly those who are judging you. I grow more and more convinced that this is the real meaning behind Jesus's famous teaching in the Sermon on the Mount, "Judge not, that you be not judged. For with the judgment you pronounce you will be judged, and with the measure you use it will be measured to you."[16] The most common interpretation I've heard is that if you act "judgy" toward others, God will use the same stiff measuring stick on you—like a paddle to the britches. That might be right but not for my money. There's no reference to divine involvement here at all. Given the whole context of the passage, I'd argue that Jesus is not speaking to you but rather all those who cannot acknowledge the legitimacy of your pain right now. I'll test this by asking a couple of questions: Do you feel judged? Does the judgment of people who don't know the details and can't fathom your situation feel fair to you? I'm guessing you'd say, "No, it doesn't." Does such ill-informed judgment inspire you to judge them in return and find them shallow, ignorant, or mean?

Well, there you go. Jesus may not be talking about divine judgment at all but merely describing what we actually do to one another in the act of passing judgment—the sorrow and pain we visit upon others when we draw final conclusions about their place, value, and worth. In the pain of your rejection, they are causing you to revisit that same scorn upon them. It's all perfectly predictable.

All these threads came together in one of the greatest tragedies of my story—the loss of our closest friends. Throughout the darkness of those ten months, Denise had confided frequently in her best friend, telling her all about my struggles and consequently hers. This friend had counseled Denise to stand up for herself and leave me. Even after Denise said this was not the right answer for her and to please stop saying it, the friend continued to do so because she maintained a right to express her own opinion. Denise began to withdraw from her because her comments were hurtful. When everything finally exploded, Denise expressed to her friend gratitude that I seemed to be on the mend and was coming back to her. The friend expressed disbelief, and in the face of the legal issues cropping up, concluded with, "He deserves everything he gets and more."

Now, she may have been right that I deserved all this and more. I do not dispute it. But Denise and I knew this friend and her husband had recently come through a series of personal struggles that nearly ended their marriage but for long and intense counseling. So of course we fulfilled Jesus's predictions and responded to her judgment with a judgment of our own—we thought her a hypocrite. I don't mean we should have or had a right to think so, only that Jesus made a true observation. We actually did what he predicted—the measuring stick she used on us, we turned around and used back on her. The practical effect of all those choices was the fracturing of the relationship, which has never been restored.

You cannot help what judgments people make about you, but if you want to survive this period with any relationships intact, I invite you to think long and hard about your own response to those judgments. Yes, go through all the emotions necessary, but pick wisely the environments where you reveal them.

I have said and say again, the bad choice that landed you here is not half so defining to your future as the choices you are making now.

CHAPTER 15

LEANING INTO
YOUR BROKENNESS

In a rejected early draft of Hawthorne's The Scarlet Letter, *Hester's pregnancy is discovered, but most of the town pretty much ignore it. The court finds her guilty of adultery, and her sentence consists of a stiff lecture amounting to "And don't do it again."*

Nevertheless, dawn arrives revealing Hester standing upon the city scaffold, a scarlet "A" stitched upon her dress by her own hand.

The villagers are abuzz with questions. What's going on? Why is she there?

A little girl tugs at her granny's sleeve, asking what it all means.

The wise old woman replies, "It is never the punishments given by others, but those we inflict upon ourselves that are the heaviest ... and the most defining."

As I FINISH THIS SECTION ON THE INITIAL FALLOUT OF YOUR crisis, I'll risk saying something hopeful. You may not be in a place to receive it yet. That's okay. As Yogi Berra said, "If you ain't where you are, you're no place." Different seasons of your experience require different parts of this book. For now, just keep reading. I think the story I'm about to tell will stick and come back to you when you're ready to hear it. God often works in such ways.

By way of context, standing before a judge in a courtroom as people say awful and sometimes even false things about you, and then having reporters pick up on those things, embellish them to make them sexier, and put them on the air as if they were settled fact—all this has a way of driving home the realization that you've pretty much wrecked your life.

That said, I'm grateful the judge in my case seemed to see through all the frenzy of the drama to the simple center, which was something like this: I had experienced a hideous lapse in judgment and made a stupid choice worthy of a teenage stoner, but I was not the menace to society others made me out to be. So rather than lock me away for many, many years, he gave me a long probation and a stack of community service hours.

We pick up our story at the Kent County Recycling Plant, which is where low-level offenders like me do their community service in our little corner of the world. This blighted job consists of standing next to a conveyer belt for eight hours at the front end of the recycling stream. A huge front-loader tractor on the ground floor dumps never-ending buckets of every possible sort of refuse onto a conveyer, which carries it to the second floor and dumps it onto another conveyor attended by twenty or so heavily supervised probationers. It's their job—it was my job—to make the first pass at pulling out everything non-recyclable. And in my eight weeks or so of laboring there, I discovered that people try to recycle some pretty ridiculous things—old car tires, bags of clothing, hunks of wood ... used diapers. Once I even pulled off a kitchen knife block, complete with the knives still in it. You can't talk to anyone else because of the noise, and no one is really interested in talking anyway.

It's the noisiest form of solitude you can imagine—a sort of fraternity of the damned, except with no sense of fraternity. The stream of garbage is never-ending. The sort of labor that would bore even Sisyphus. It does, however, give you a lot of time to think, and perhaps that's part of the point.

Being a Protestant, the idea of penance never took up much space in my theology. But now I began to wonder more about the value it might have. As I stood there on sore flat feet, dragging the detritus of environmental zealots off the conveyer, the idea of doing something with the body to express remorse for the sins of the soul didn't seem like such a silly idea. So I made a bargain with myself. I would spend each four-hour shift contemplating some specific person or group I had wronged in my folly. The morning shift might consist of intentional reflection on the elders at the church and the afternoon shift on my former dean at the seminary. These were people who had to pick up the mess I'd left behind.

I spent a shift reflecting on my students at the seminary, another thinking about what all this had done to my kids, and two whole shifts thinking about my wife, who was the most innocent and most greatly wronged party in the whole sorry business. As I neared the end, I was even able to experience enough remorse to spend a shift thinking about the wrong I'd done to Lorelai—a particularly humbling experience given that I was also still angry over the many wrongs she had done me in the ten preceding months.

Nothing drives home the egregious nature of one's combat errors than reflecting on the names of the dead and wounded. By the time my community service hours were winding down, I was in a pretty low state. I was convinced my imbecility was so great that not only would I never be given another chance to do anything worthwhile but I didn't even deserve such a chance. I was like the garbage on the belt before me—cast off, unwanted. Less useful than even a piece of glass or plastic that would travel down the belt and eventually (through some miracle I still don't understand) be given a new usefulness by the recycling process.

No, I was just one of the pieces of unsalvageable flotsam that got dragged off at the first stage and sent down the chute, destined for the landfill.

As I was ruminating on this dark prospect, my gloved hand fell upon a piece of unrecyclable gray plastic. By rote I pulled it free from the stream and held it over the garbage chute. Only then did my eyes register what it was. Some environmentally conscious citizen had decided to recycle a shattered resin lawn ornament. At one time it had probably been a St. Francis, but now all that was left on the recycling stream was an eight-inch piece of his robed legs. It wasn't even obvious this was what it was till I made out the small cross hanging from his waist. I stood staring at this piece of shattered saint as the leftover debris of an enlightened civilization coursed past me on the conveyer.

Then it struck me. This was a metaphor for the whole thing. Once a respected member of the community of saints, now shattered in pieces and consigned to the rubbish heap.

At least that was what was about to happen. Old St. Francis hovered over the trash chute while I sorted out what I was feeling. He had no value to anyone. He'd already been thrown away once. He served no purpose anymore. He was destined for the landfill. Unless … unless the one holding him refused to let go. And for all his woes, he *was* still being held by someone.

In that moment, it seemed to me that my own destiny hung on what I did next.

The rules had been made clear. Nothing was to be removed from the building under penalty of law. But the reason I was there in the first place was for ignoring the law, so I supposed it was time to live up to the reputation I'd been branded with. I secreted St. Francis in my sock and wore him home like a holy shin guard. He now hangs on the wall of my study, reminding me that while broken things are often discarded, not always. Sometimes they get recycled. The difference lies in the worth they have to the one holding them.

You can be shattered to the point where you don't see any value in yourself anymore. Your friends or family may have abandoned you. The whole culture may have dismissed you based on what little it thinks it knows. All this hurts like hell. But remember, ultimately, you do not lie in any of these hands. You are held in the hands of Another. One who does not discard, but shattered though you are, calls you a saint—not because your actions have always been saintly but because Another's holy actions have been credited to your account.

All who rest upon that Savior's actions are called saints because of him. And for him, it doesn't matter how many pieces you've been smashed into. For him, nothing goes down the chute, because for him everything is useful, everything can be recycled. So hang on. My story doesn't end here.

Neither does yours.

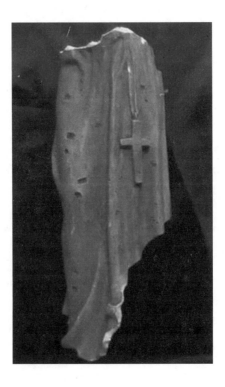

PART 3

FINDING NEWNESS

Perspectives for Starting Over and Finding Hope

Everybody has their moment of great opportunity in life. If you happen to miss the one you care about, then everything else becomes eerily easy.

—Douglas Adams, *Mostly Harmless*

Coming Out of Hiding

He was an odd child. Not because his face was deformed by that accident in infancy—that was mere tragedy. No, he was odd because of ... well, the other thing.

His parents didn't know what to do. His older siblings showed no sign of his condition. They, like most children, were afraid of the dark. At bedtime, they demanded nightlights, comforting stories, and flashlights shined under the bed.

But the youngest ...

He eagerly went to bed every night and demanded perfect darkness. But every morning he had to be dragged bodily from his room. For unlike his siblings, long brooding over his wrecked face had made him afraid of coming into the light.

B REW-HA-HA, A COFFEE SHOP ON THE MAIN DRAG A MILE north of the seminary, had been my perennial hangout. I went there to grade papers, write, or just think. I often ran into students and occasionally other faculty from the university. The owner Kevin knew me by name and knew my drinks—a pour over of the bean-du-jour with room for cream till I'd filled the punch card, then I'd splurge on his largest latte.

After the news coverage, I couldn't go back. The thought of walking into a place where I would be recognized by former students and colleagues was unbearable. I just hid at home for eight months till the public moved on to some sexier story.

At some point, wearied of rattling around in my house, I determined to reenter the domain of men. I don't know how I decided Brew-ha-ha would be my Heartbreak Ridge, but I found myself in front of the shop. I sat in my car for five minutes, ginning up the courage to get out. Did I really need to do this? What was I trying to prove?

I wouldn't now defend the following thoughts, but I'm trying to describe them honestly, because such an emergence is coming for you to. And whether or not it's right, playing the victim inside your own head may be the only way to get through it.

As I sat there twiddling my car keys, something snapped deep down in the clockworks, like little Ralphie Parker going out of his skull on Scut Farkus's face in *A Christmas Story*. Darn it! This was *my* coffee shop. This was *my* hangout. They'd taken everything else; they were *not* going to get this too. I was going to reclaim my tiny fiefdom, and the Scut Farkuses of the world best beware.

I was bruising for a confrontation. I'd spent almost a year suppressing every instinct and desire for vindication, and part of me was just itching for someone to look at me cross-eyed so I could cuss them out. So donning every piece of emotional armor I possessed—the helmet of stoicism, the breastplate of indignation, and the shield of "Whatchu lookin' at?"—I sallied forth into the dragon's lair.

I stepped through the door and looked around defiantly, expecting to lock eyes with some familiar face. Well, I did. Kevin's. He was plying his Columbian fair trade behind the machine. His face went wide with surprise and something else I didn't recognize. He killed the steam and charged out from behind the counter like the proverbial bull seeing red. On the bridge of my mind, Captain Kirk was yelling red alert because every retort had left me. I was defenseless against whatever was about to happen, and I think I even turned to leave.

Before I could grab the door handle, however, Kevin had my paw in his own and was pumping it up and down as if he expected me to produce water—and I almost did. It took me a second to understand what he was saying. Over and over, he burbled, "Jeremy, it's so good to see you. You are welcome here. So welcome ..."

He led me to a booth and sat me down. I think he even gave me a complimentary cup of coffee—something he was notorious for *not* doing, margins being what they are in small indie coffee shops.

I don't remember saying anything for the first ten minutes as he launched into a story of his own failed marriage, conflicts with his adult children, and every other personal failing that had dominated his recent past. As I wondered what it was about my face that made me look like a priest, he climaxed with, "So, Jeremy, we're *all* just ragamuffins! You know that? All of us. You're no different. It's all grace, all of it. There's nothing else."

He asked how I was doing. He asked about my family. He asked what I needed. He asked about the support structures in my life.

He did not ask me to clarify the story. He did not ask me if what was in the paper was true. He did not probe me about any of the thousand painful details of the journey, to fill in the gaps. He was perfectly incurious about everything other than my well-being.

He wanted me to know I was loved, that I had worth, that I was welcome.

The most difficult thing he asked—even though he said it gently and told me up front it was okay not to answer or even have an answer—was, "Have you reached a point where you can thank God for it yet?"

This was a singularly annoying question and the closest he came to getting biffed in the nose. Before I could clench my fist, however, he rattled back into his own story of loss and the changes in perspective that accompanied every step of it. His bold question had been trying to draw out the principle that not all steps in the journey look the same. It changes as you progress. Your own thoughts about it change. I had no answer for his actual question at the time, but it was a pivotal moment for me. Questions I didn't know existed or even needed answering began to percolate.

What about you? Some time has passed since the explosion —a few months or years. Something like a new normal—whether you like it or not—is beginning to impose itself. It's not crisis anymore—it's beginning to just feel like "life." You're growing a little numb to your losses—your family, your reputation, your career, your self-respect—but some new things have begun to emerge too, like a new job, a new apartment, a new hobby to kill the hours, new rhythms.

Perhaps it's time for you to also begin probing the next layer of questions. *Who am I? Where am I going now? What are God and I going to do with each other?*

The First of Its Kind

Kevin was the first person in eight months to say anything like that to me—the first to suggest there was something next for me. Caveat: I mean he was the first "ordinary" person—not a clerical person discharging some pastoral office, but the first person who didn't *have* to say what he said. Caveat the second: A number of people—a few from the church specifically—had invited us to dinner or to their swimming pool or made other tangible gestures of love. I don't mean to minimize those generous and grace-filled acts. But Kevin was the first person wholly unconnected to my story who had expressed all this to me ... and he didn't have to. It *felt* like the first grace I'd received, or maybe the first grace I was able to receive. It was the one that broke the shell. All others were perhaps preparatory and played their part, but his was the one that stuck. Some had planted, some had watered—sadly, some had only fertilized—but Kevin was the one who saw the fruit.

That's when I knew I was ready to take some tentative steps toward rebuilding. That's the moment I knew it would be all right. I knew I would make it. I didn't know what the future looked like, but for the first time, I actually believed there would be one.

The vagabond Cain had settled in the land of Nod and now wondered what was next for him. This final section of this book deals with Cain rebuilding. How do you live with the memories, the shame, the isolation that come from having a backstory like ours? What does resurrection look like for people whose death came by suicide? How do we move from the realm of loss to a posture of expectant hope?

I can't tell you when it's time for you to step into this space. You probably won't be able to predict it or see it coming. One day you'll just wake up and feel a bit more like yourself than you did yesterday. Or perhaps you'll have a Brew-ha-ha moment, and it will persuade you that it's time. That conversation will break through the haze and gloom. For me, it was the first beam of sunrise falling on eyes starved for light. Night withdrew before his gentle and genial optimism, confirming to me that darkness is not the opposite of light ... but only the absence of it.

CHAPTER 17

LIVING WITH SHAME

Goofus the simpleton was giving his friend a tour of his new house. Upon entering the master bath, the friend stopped and stared at the blank wall over the sink. "Good heavens, where's the mirror?"

"Oh," sneered Goofus, "I got rid of that thing."

"Why? Didn't fit the decor?"

"No, it creeped me out. No matter what I tried, this ugly man kept showing up in it to watch everything I did."

DENISE AND I USED TO BE ABLE TO FIGHT LIKE MARRIED people. By that I mean we'd both state our positions, disagree, sometimes resolve the issue, sometimes get huffy. We're not really yellers by nature, but we can both get pretty intense about our sides. If we had individual faults, mine was I tended to repeat my case in new words over and over till I extracted weary agreement. In short, I badgered. Denise tended to make her argument in terms of a failure. That is, she shamed.

When things blew up, we had almost twenty years of marriage under our belts. We'd both spent a lot of time working on our respective faults, and we knew the other's well enough to sort of deal with them. She generally ignored my badgering, and I ignored her blaming.

Then I screwed up, and that all changed.

Now we have trouble fighting. Through our dark journey, she developed a stronger, more independent self. So she was pretty well done with letting me restate my case endlessly, piling analogy atop analogy like a reanimated C. S. Lewis. She started telling me when I'd made my point and needed to stop talking.

Something had changed in me too. For the first time in my life, I really had something for which I held most all the blame. So almost overnight, her strategy of blaming, which she'd nearly outgrown, became deadly to me. The remnants of that habit, combined with her newfound liberty to silence me when she'd had enough, left me rhetorically impotent.

I had learned something new. I had learned shame.

Shame Versus Guilt

Shame and *guilt* are often used interchangeably, and that's fine for most conversations. Here, however, it won't do. I need to distinguish them. I use *guilt* in its legal sense, that objective state of having done wrong, blameworthiness, or culpability. It's that dark mark credited to your moral ledger by having done the deed— regardless of how you feel about it.

Shame, on the other hand, is a feeling. It's that horrible sense of humiliation, remorse, and self-loathing that follows on the heels of having done the deed. It's the subjective awareness of having failed some standard or having been found unworthy.

Now, using these two words in this way, it's easy to see how they relate to each other. Shame ought to follow guilt. If one is objectively guilty of murder or theft, one ought to feel a subjective sense of shame over it. The corollary is true as well—if you've done nothing wrong, you ought to feel no shame. At least that's how it's supposed to work.

We all know cases, however, where one is present without the other, and it clearly mucks up things. The murderer who feels no remorse or the rapist who feels no regret is appalling to us. They are an advanced case of what St. Paul calls "a seared conscience,"[17] people who can't even tell their own deeds are evil—the acts don't *feel* evil to them.

The opposite situation also arises, as in the case of the young child whose parents are divorcing and though guilty of no fault, he is eaten up by shame about it. Or the young woman standing before the dissembling mirror feeling shame and self-loathing over her genetic endowment—one of the least blameworthy things a person has. Such people have no legitimate cause for shame yet *feel* it anyway. The apostle may have had this in view when he spoke of "weaker brothers"[18]—those whose consciences are so tender that they misfire, go off too easily, giving them a sense of being wrong where no wrong has been done.

While both of these permutations are unfortunate, our response to them is obvious. I don't mean it's easy to help either individual. I mean, rather, that we have a sense of the direction in which the solution lies.

In the case of incorrigible criminals, we lock them up in prisons because allowing people with defective moral compasses to walk the streets freely is a danger to everyone including themselves. In the case of tender, shame-filled innocents, we send them to therapy, hoping wise counselors will help them deal with their misplaced terrors.

I don't mean to oversimplify either case. I know it's more complicated than this. I only present this reduction to bracket it away and ask about the much harder case—my case, your case.

What do we do with the person who *deserves* the shame they feel?

What do we do with people like you and me who, having done the awful thing, now feel awful about it? Is such shame something to be gotten past? If the shame is deserved, would it be right to try to liberate me from it? Why does a robust view of the gospel seem to preach both genuine moral guilt with its consequent shame *and* a liberation from that same guilt-shame?

The Burden of Justified Shame

To answer this question, we need to appreciate just how big a problem shame is for those with self-inflicted wounds. If you've never had to operate out of a place of deep shame, I don't know how to explain how debilitating it is. For one thing, it's hard to feel shame *only* for what one did wrong. Shame, like a chill in the night, creeps.

A man rises in the morning, looks into the bathroom mirror, and hates the reflection he finds there. What exactly is the connection between his shame and that reflection? None, really. It's just the face of a person so many years old who just rolled out of bed. Yet he's filled with such self-loathing that he's frequently tempted to punch the glass just to blot out that face. Why?

Shame metastasizes. It doesn't stay put. It refuses to stay attached to the offense in the past. It expands out from the epicenter of that fault till it spreads an oily residue over a whole life. It reaches backward, destroying the past. It stretches forward into every possible future. In my case, it caused me to question every good work I'd ever done at the seminary and church—every lecture, every sermon, every meeting with a weeping troubled student. It felt as though everything I'd ever done was now worthless and without merit. This feeling seemed to be confirmed when the university immediately scrubbed the website of any trace I had ever been there. People at the church were asking whether they should take down the audio of my sermons from the church website. When your past has been delegitimized, and your present is pointless, what hope is there for the future?

Shame paralyzes. It means when you're having a fight with your wife about unloading the dishwasher, and she says she's tired of doing it because she's "the one who's doing most of the cleaning," you lose the power to reply, "I loaded the damn thing yesterday, darling." No, even though that's true, you can't say it. You just collapse into sullen silence. Why? Because so many years ago, you were clinically depressed, and she really *did* do most all the cleaning for months on end—as well as everything else that kept the family running.

But then your wife assures you that she wasn't even referring to those events so many years ago. That was the furthest thing from her mind. She was only talking about the past couple of days. No matter—you're in the grip of shame. You know that at some point this argument *was* true. You did fail. You did let the family down. And by means of some dark magic, this discussion today has become a continuation of your screwing up.

That's what shame does. It makes you forever guilty not only of the thing you actually did but of every other possible shortcoming that crosses your path. *If I can be guilty of something as horrible as an emotional betrayal of my spouse, then, yes, I am probably the sort of person who wouldn't do his share of the housework.* It fits the profile. Shame makes you guilty of all possible faults.

How Shall We Then Live?
What to Do with Shame

Can you see shame's blessing and its danger? A blessing in that feelings of shame can be the mirror that forces us to reckon with our actual sins—and thus is a precursor to experiencing forgiveness. It's a form of penitence. Only people who are sorry endure it. Those who blithely dismiss and evade their wrongs do not feel shame. The danger is that it opens us up to new forms of self-deception and despair. It all depends on what you do with it.

One of the bad things you can do with it is to simply pray for its removal. Does it surprise you that I say this? Surely, you say, we should seek liberation from anything that makes us feel bad, right? I'm no longer so sure we should. Even shame may serve a higher purpose. There might be lessons you're supposed to be learning from it. I don't know the use God intends to make of shame in your life, and consequently, how should I know whether to pray for its removal? I think the truth is harder and better than that.

Christianity teaches us to confess sin, believing in the objective remission of *guilt* available through the life, death, and resurrection of Christ. Christianity speaks of God's generous and forgiving nature in Christ. It says, however, much less about the remission of shame. When the Scripture speaks of shame at all, it most often speaks not of its *removal* but of its *covering*, as if you can hold a very serviceable view of forgiveness and still feel shame—as if the goal is not its elimination but its guarded investiture into some sacred corner of the soul.

This tells me that the lingering form of shame may be a necessary part of the journey for such as you and me. Thus, even if I had the power to take it magically from you in a moment (a power no one has), I would do so only to your harm. Like so many other negatives we experience in life, the feeling of shame is also an invitation—not to run away and hide but to stand up and embrace it, to look it in the eyes and understand it's part of who you are now.

> You can hold a very serviceable view of forgiveness and still feel shame—as if the goal is not its elimination but its guarded investiture into some sacred corner of the soul.

As one of the Bright People says in C. S. Lewis's *The Great Divorce*, "Shame is like that. If you will accept it—if you will drink the cup to the bottom—you will find it very nourishing: but try to do anything else with it and it scalds."[19] You do not heal from deserved shame. You do not outlive it. You do not delete it. You make the choice to inhabit it and to allow it to inhabit you. As with other forms of pain, you must let it do the holy work only it can do.

It is a deep dark brush stroke across the canvas of your life. There it is. It's not coming off. There is no eraser. There is no going back to the painting as it existed before that horrific slash of paint marred your beautiful portrait. On pain of despair, the question cannot be *How do I get rid of it?* Rather, you can only ask whether that stroke will remain a mere slash of wreckage.

Might there instead be a way to lean into it—incorporate it into the total portrait?

Bob Ross often made such great marring strokes across his seemingly finished paintings. He called them "happy little accidents." I recoil from the phrase in this context. It trivializes the horror of our experience, but it also makes an important point. After ruining his beautiful landscape with a great slash of brown down the middle, he would then go on to incorporate it into the whole as a pine tree or log, a slash of blue as a lake, a slash of white as a cloud. Often these *accidents* would come to dominate the foreground, changing the nature and focus of the picture in ways you would not have thought possible.

I think our lives are a bit like that. A man who destroys his marriage but then owns the behavior that did it goes on to have a successful marriage of twenty years and becomes an elder in his church. A teenager who believes her eating disorder has ruined her life fights on and becomes a riveting vegan food critic. Another man leaves the state penitentiary, his sentence completed, and starts an inner city church ministering to the homeless and broken in ways only he can. These are not imaginary examples. I know each of these people. I have watched them slowly, diligently incorporate the great slash in their painting in ways that unexpectedly enhance its beauty.

Yes, your sin, your betrayal, your crime, your mistake, whatever it was, changes the focus of your painting forever. That can't be helped. You've already made the stroke. But what that stroke means to the total landscape has not yet been determined. Your painting is not yet finished. Get out your brushes. You have more work to do.

Keep this thought before you, because what is true of shame will be true of much that is to follow. Yes, a new and unsettling color you did not plan on using in this painting has now been added to your palette. The question remains, What use will you make of it?

CHAPTER 18

LIVING WITH
A SENSE OF FAILURE

As his retirement party wound down, the man sat, brooding over his cocktail. It had been a remarkable run—founding a humanitarian agency, becoming a senator, then a college president, then a philanthropist.

"I wonder what my dad would think of me now," he mused dejectedly.

His companion was shocked. "Are you kidding? Look at all you've done. What more could a father desire from a son?"

"Yes, I know, but I think he wanted me to become a librarian like him."

I HAD THREE GREAT MENTORS IN MY LIFE. THE FIRST WAS MY advisor in seminary—Uncle Joe, we called him. He died in 2000 as I was finishing work on my master's degree. In fact, one of the last things he did before unexpectedly shuffling off this mortal coil was grade the rough draft of my thesis. I got it back with a note saying something like, "Well done. Any additional edits you make will not affect the grade. Passed: A."

A week later, he was gone. It's like he knew it was coming. I've often wondered if my thesis was somehow responsible for

148

his death—*like it was so bad it killed him!* When graduation rolled around, the dean asked me my status. I showed him the draft with its hand-scrawled note. The dean looked lost. Clearly they don't train you for such eventualities at dean school. He shrugged and approved me for graduation. No final draft, no defense, no revisions or edits. I felt both relieved and cheated at the same time. But what's a dean to do?

The second of the great ones, Dr. Jim, was also one of my seminary professors. He died while I was in the throes of my darkness. I didn't even go to his funeral because I was headed out of town and wanted to get settled into my hotel as quickly as possible so I could resume texting Lorelai. What madness!

Well, it was worth it in terms of the immediate twisted goals. That was the night she first expressed a desire for me to "be with her." After a particularly florid series of texts, the line as I remember it popped up, "It's a good thing you're not here right now." Which set up a chain reaction of feelings in me—everything from a Monty Python-esque "Run away, run away!" to "I can be there in an hour." Of course, her offer wasn't sincere—it never was—but what does that matter when you enjoy the mere titillation of the idea just as much? What an idiot!

I tell this story to emphasize what a useless creature I'd become in the face of my beloved mentor's death. I had already stood at his hospice bedside and, like an arrogant fool, responded to his concerns for the future with something like, "Don't worry, we'll take it from here," meaning he had run his race well and it was now time for me to start carrying the water. And immediately after leaving his bedside, I burst into tears and shared my grief not with Denise but with Lorelai—texting all the way to the car, where I lost the hospice home's Wi-Fi signal. What an ass!

It took me more than six years to build up the moxie to stand before his grave, wiping the snow from the stone and pouring out a useless apology with many tears. That day I discovered Uncle Joe was buried in the same cemetery—a mere hundred feet further up the hill. So I had to have a come-to-Jesus moment with him too.

My third mentor was my college advisor and friend, Robes, who made it till Christmas 2017 before passing without warning in his sixties. I went to his funeral and grieved, less over his passing and more about why I had not contacted him once in the years since my losses. Not gotten his advice. Not sought any comfort or help. No "Tuesdays with Robesie." Now I'll never have the chance.

Why didn't I reach out to Robes? What draws me back to Dr. Jim's and Uncle Joe's gravestones periodically to weep? What drives such self-recrimination? If you have self-inflicted wounds, I don't have to tell you. You already know. It's that horrible shame discussed in the previous chapter, yes, but now sprinkled with a particularly pungent spice—the knowledge that you've failed those whose opinion mattered to you.

Disappointed Whom?

To persons who felt they had promise, who spent their lives preparing to do something great, who'd had others—great people—invest in them beyond their desert, the knowledge of having blown it is soul-crushing. What makes it so horrific is that there is no denying it. It is true. Whatever visions those three men had of what I would do with their investment, I'm sure it didn't include writing this book.

When it comes to such things, the dead wield more power over us than the living. It ominously revises the old Steve Green song that talks about how those who come after us should find us faithful into *What if those who went before us could see us now?*[20] You've seen the memes, I'm sure—the twenty-year-old millennial wearing a puppy-dog Instagram filter contrasted with the twenty-year-old from 1944 taking German gunfire on a Normandy beach. The contrast is selective and unfair, and yet deep inside us, a somewhat comparable insecurity shouts that we don't quite measure up to the expectation of some great one in our past—a rigid father, an inspiring teacher, an overbearing God.

There it is—the elephant!

Disappointing God is of course the central problem, because every mentor was merely human. They didn't know us perfectly. They never really knew what we were capable of or what we were *here for*. They were just guessing—doing their best. And rightly so. That's all any of us can do with our charges, whether children, students, congregants, or employees. We are finite and fallible, so our expectations of others are themselves finite and fallible. God, however, is neither. God knows us thoroughly, knows what gifts and burdens we carry, knows the good and evil of which we are really capable. In short, God knows perfectly what we might have been. So therein lies the final burden—How are we to deal with the suspicion that we've disappointed the God who knew what we were *supposed* to be?

A Nonanswer

I suppose one way to answer is just to ignore all the data and say nice things—God is loving, God is forgiving, God understands, God isn't displeased, upset, or angry. We'd be fine if we could just have a God who experiences no disappointment or never has negative attitudes toward us.

Evidence aside, such a God would not be compelling to people like me. When you've done real damage and someone replies with, "Oh, it's no big deal. Nobody really minds," it rings false. Scripture is full of descriptions of people who pleased God and people who didn't. It seems pure sophistry to say, "God just loves everybody," if by that you also mean, "God doesn't mind what anybody does." It's incredible to say God is fine with Adam eating apples, Moses whacking rocks, Samson getting a shave, or David ... well, doing all that murder and adultery stuff. No,

God is not pleased by this, and we are fools to assert divine favor where evil has been done.

I did evil—systematically, repeatedly, and post-conversion. I rebelled with the same ferocity as Judas's betrayal, Peter's denial, and Thomas's doubt. If God *doesn't* have a problem with what I did, then there is something wrong with God. Such a God is neither good nor holy. All hope of distinguishing good and evil goes out the window if God does not in some meaningful sense *disapprove*. Therefore, on pain of idiocy, we must assert divine displeasure when it is merited, even if we happen to be the objects.

The only people who can avoid this question are either those who've never thought deeply about it or have never had to live with deep, spine-curving guilt. My soul hourly demands an answer—What precisely does God think and feel about what I did? And assuming it's negative, how am I to live with that?

I'm Sorry, but ... Theology

I think a little heavy lifting is unavoidable at this point. For questions like the ones I'm asking, simple answers don't work. The data is complicated and requires a little sleuthing.

To be clear, I am not questioning whether God forgives when I repent. That's a given. I accept that when I repented, God forgave. God and I are reconciled. The struggle I'm having regards the lingering heartburn of *having* disappointed God—the human crisis of knowing I failed God. I broke covenant. I am a Christian who went morally apostate. God has forgiven me, but how can I endure the memory of the failure and the knowledge of how God *felt* about it?

Surely David had already repented and been forgiven before he wrote Psalms 32 and 51, and yet he felt compelled to write them anyway—as if though knowing he'd been forgiven, he still had to wrestle with a kind of hangover from having failed God.

He seems to struggle with the idea that he caused God some sort of negative *feeling*.

So here are the brazen questions: What *did* God think or feel when you and I did our awful thing? And what does it even mean for God to *think* or *feel* disappointment, displeasure, and other negative emotions?

I know two ways of getting a coherent answer. One comes from the Bible and the other from the theologians, and I happen to think they're both true. But you can decide for yourself.

An Answer from the Bible: Failure versus Tested and Approved

After examining all the major passages in the Bible that discuss God's pleasure/displeasure (in both English and the original languages), I find two major ideas at work.[21]

First, God's pleasure over righteousness and displeasure over unrighteousness are real things. This is the bad news. What we fear to be the case really is. What God finds *acceptable, pleasing*, and *favorable* is exactly what we thought. God delights in us when we, for example, trust, act justly, and keep God's commandments. God is pleased with righteous acts and behavior and is displeased with the other kind.

There's no honest way around it. When I screwed up, God was displeased and disappointed. God detests sin. It's a breach of the peace God intended for the world. Furthermore, nothing I found in the biblical language distinguishes between my *actions* and *me*—as in "God hates sin but is fine with sinners." This matches our own experience. Just as it's useless to say, "I'm disappointed in my child's actions but not in my child." You may mean something by that distinction, but it's meaningless to your child. If God is hiding behind such a flimsy nuance ("I'm disappointed in your choice but not you"), it is shabby comfort for

Cain's children. "The water is putrid, but the well is fine" is an irrelevant distinction to thirsty men.

No, it is specific people—like Enoch, Jesus, good servants, those with faith—who are pleasing to and find favor with God. By definition, then, it must be specific people—like the Lord's killers, the unbelieving Israelites in the wilderness ... Jeremy Gordon Grinnell—who forfeit it.

If we find it a horrible thing to have disappointed God, then the proper response is not to deny the biblical witness but to sin less. It's better for the child to recognize that her conduct displeases her parent and amend her ways than to try to live in the fiction, *Oh, my parents don't feel displeasure, only love.* I confess this fills me with fear and reinforces all my heartbreak, but truth is always beneficial, always life-giving, even when it hurts.

So lest you lose hope, the New Testament makes a second point. God's pleasure is also expressed at our having been *judged, tested,* or *approved* by a trial or struggle—that we've come through it well.[22] These are less emotive and more evaluative terms.

Throughout the Epistles, we're told that we (that is, our faith, our spirits, our minds, our proclamation, and so on) are being formed by our experiences. Hard times, temptations, tragedies, and threats both from within and without seek our destruction, but the Father is faithful to bring his children through them—and not just by skins-of-teeth. Rather, when endured with constancy, such trials and tribulations form, shape, and purify us the way gold is purified. Having passed through the fire, we are now pure, holy, and pleasing to God.

Do you see the point? Yes, it's true that when we screwed up, in some real sense we hurt the heart of God. That's what evil does. But now we learn that even screwups like you and me are given another chance. Even—perhaps especially—for those of us whose wounds are self-inflicted and whose burdens are self-imposed, God does not define us by that failure. Even now as you bear up under the consequences, your character and faith are being tested, formed, tempered. We can still please and delight God in how we handle our current struggle—the struggle that is even now shaping and molding us. St. Paul makes the point to the Philippian church, "Forgetting what is behind and straining toward what is ahead, I press on toward the goal to win the prize for which God has called me heavenward in Christ Jesus."[23] Remember, Paul had a lot to put behind him, so he knew what he was talking about.

When we own our failures, embrace with humility the consequences, amend our conduct, and allow divine grace to do its work, we are pleasing to God. God is pleased with and favors us. That is how the Bible speaks, and as such, must reflect something true about God's attitude toward me. Insofar as I have worked through my failures sufficiently to now write a book to help others—and I can only accept this as an act of faith—I am pleasing to God. God is pleased with me in this labor, for it shows I have been tested and tempered and have in some sense become approved, "a worker who [no longer needs] to be ashamed."[24] I need to be reminded of that ... daily.

The Answer from Theologians: Eternity and the Divine Feels

That is how the Bible speaks of God, and so I feel confident that using such language is good, wholesome, and right. And yet it raises some longstanding questions about what God is like. What does it mean for God to *feel* at all?

I don't pretend to know what it means for a God who is Spirit to *feel* an emotion, any emotion—joy or displeasure—anymore than I understand what it means for a Spirit without a brain to *think* a thought. Scripture speaks *as if* God has thoughts and feelings, and so I accept that this is true of God. Even if such language is only analogy or accommodation, it says something real though perhaps unpicturable about God's experience. So be it.

THE BELLOWING *of* CAIN

But if as the theologians tell us, God is eternal and all-knowing, then God isn't just looking at me at this moment, "feeling" whatever is warranted of me *now*. Rather, every moment of my life is *NOW* before God—known with completeness in God's complete *NOW*.

Therefore, something like the following must also be true: God's attitude toward me is one singular thing. It incorporates all the data of my whole life—past, present, future. The pleasure and displeasure of God, the wrath under which I lay prior to my conversion, the redemptive love that dominates the relationship after, the joy of my complete redemption yet to come—all this is present in God's *NOW*.

So when I return to the Scriptures and discover they say I am beloved, I'm presented with a mystery of faith. By the terms of the deal, such a statement must include my time of rebellion and apostasy. That is, *I am beloved* is an eternal fact. It is not an eternal fact *in spite of* my sin and rebellion but by their inclusion. God's love somehow incorporates even my most loathsome failures! It boggles the imagination.

> God's love somehow incorporates even my most loathsome failures!

It breathes new meaning into St. Paul's question, "What can separate us from the love of God?" His answer is clear, "Nothing created,"[25] which is to say that nothing in this whole time-space reality can alter the perspective of the eternal *NOW* in which I am called "beloved."

This does not undo in the least the scandal of my rebellion or the egregiousness of my offense. But it does tell me who I am *in the face of them*. My apostasy did not surprise God or give rise to a divine reassessment of my case.

God knows perfectly well from the eternal *NOW* that your story includes this ugly chapter, and yet God calls you "beloved" in the very face of it.

How Shall We Then Live? An Analogy of a Lost Son

The story of the prodigal son is not best understood as that of a father raving with perpetual anger toward his departed son, who then, upon seeing him, experiences an unexpected softening and on *that* basis, runs out and embraces him. No, the only way to coherently read that narrative is that of a father constantly pacing his rooftop, actively looking for a day he already knows is coming—a day when his son's repentance will catch up with the love and forgiveness already present in his father. The father's disappointment, anger, forgiveness, and desire for his son are all present together *before* the son arrives at the gate. All of these in their totality make up the father's love for his son. The analogy is imperfect, of necessity being told of a human father, but the impact is substantially correct.

All of this yields the following truth: You and I—vagabonds, ragamuffins, and wastrels—are beloved not by the exclusion of our disappointing moments but somehow, in the eternal life of God, by their inclusion. God does not love despite; God *is* love and loves in the full knowledge of our failures.

Faith—if it is to be faith—asks me to take God at God's word. If, in full knowledge of my apostasy, God has called me beloved, then I can either continue to persecute myself with the question needlessly or embrace the divine declaration ... and find rest.

CHAPTER 19

LIVING WITH THE LOSSES

Two butterflies, having just emerged from their cocoons, were drying their damp wings in the morning sun. They were not equally pleased with their transformations.

"Imagine," said one, "never again being able to crawl along a branch ... "

"But—" began the other, spreading her wings.

"Or chewing green leaves ... "

"But—"

"And remember those lovely stripes we used to have."

"But—"

"Hang it all! It's like all the best parts of being a caterpillar have been stolen away. What are we supposed to do now? Why can't we just be like we were before?"

He got no argument from the other this time ... for she had flown away.

A FEW MONTHS AFTER ALL THE HR STUFF AT THE SEMI-nary was resolved, I scheduled lunch with Gary, my former dean. He hadn't been allowed to have any contact with me till then, but I wanted to apologize to him for the tsunami of horrors I'd let loose on him. He was a model of forgiveness and grace, and for the next few years we would get together for an annual lunch to catch up. Well, at some point I realized there was a question I had never actually voiced, but I sensed I needed to if I was really to move on.

So when we next got together for lunch (our last, actually), I brought him up to speed on all God had been doing in my life and family—including that now, some six years after the explosion, I had reached a place where I wondered what the future might hold for me. At that point in the conversation, I uttered my question for which I already knew the answer.

"Can you see any possibility, in any possible world, where I might ever be allowed to stand at the front of a classroom again at the university—in *any* capacity?" That seemed a question with sufficient caveats to admit some light between the cracks, if any were to be had.

His answer, as I expected, was no, but for reasons that surprised me. He made two points—one administrative and one personal. He insisted that, from an administrative perspective, when an institution has had to release someone in such a manner, there is no way for them ever to reengage that person without opening the institution to legal risk from every other person who's ever been let go. I had not thought of this angle. But it fits. Remember David Mamet's maxim, "It is the artist's job to create. It is the institution's job to continue." Risk mitigation is the most deeply held value of the American institution. It just is. It's no good denying it or whining about it. It will act to preserve itself from threats.

Okay, fine.

What came next, however, shocked me. "Jeremy, you were one of the best classroom professors I'd ever seen. That's what made your, uh … situation so hard. And given all you've been through, I have no doubt you'd be even better at it now. Unfortunately, someone else will have to benefit from all that growth."

That I might again be allowed to teach students *somewhere, someday* should have been an encouraging thing to hear, except I already knew it offered no hope. Six months earlier I had learned of a position at a small college in the South that looked like it had been designed just for me—professor of systematics, emphasis on doctrines of humanity and sin, high classroom skills, low administrative duties. I was made aware of it by a friend who had gone to school with several of the committee faculty. He contacted them on my behalf and told them about this guy he knew who was the perfect institutional fit ... only he had this one problem. They listened patiently and agreed that I sounded like a great fit, but with fifty applications from nonfelons on their desk already, it just wasn't "worth the risk." Oh, David Mamet, you prophet—the artist must take risks; the institution must not.

A week later I was having coffee with a former student and successful business owner—a real go-getter, type-A, sweet, wonderful man who would give you the shirt off his back. I was rehearsing this chain of events and expressing a little bitterness at the irony of having "learned so much no one wants you"—a criminal case of over-qualification.

He listened and replied, "With God all things are possible."

"Not this."

"Don't say that! God can do anything, even this."

What was I to say? Really? It's possible for me to be a college professor of theology again? In this world? I knew the deep and sincere place from which his words had come, but I still wanted to box his ears.

Enough with the BS Already

Here's the problem with that form of "encouragement." It's false. Biblically and existentially false. Not false in the sense that God is *not* all-powerful or capable of redeeming evil into good but false in that the naiveté it represents about God's management of the world is almost as destructive as the evil it seeks to address.

Let's cut to the chase. You know how many truly redemptive

stories are in the Bible? Stories of people who fail and then upon taking their redemptive journey, find themselves in a comparable position to what they had before they screwed up?

One. Two at best.

"What?" you say. "There are lots!"

Really? Name them.

Cain is the archetype, but don't forget his father, Adam, who doesn't get the garden back. Moses loses the promised land. Saul loses his kingdom. Penitent David keeps his throne, but his life becomes a perpetual hellhole. Judas's repentance comes too late or is insincere or offered to the wrong person, and he suicides. I could go on—Lot, Samson, Gideon, Jephthah, Simon Magus, Ananias and Sapphira. Even the prophets, who speak endlessly of a great restoration to the land for exiled Israel, hold a dirty little secret left unsaid in most sermons. The people to whom the promises of return are given will die in exile. Not they but their grandchildren will be the ones to reenter the land.

Tell me again of the great restorative acts of God.

In most cases—repentant or not—people who mess up suffer all the consequences of their actions unremitted and, though forgiven and brought back into relationship with God, never get back anything comparable to what they threw away.

I said this is true with one or two exceptions, and I'll come to them in a minute. But first we have to face this hard reality—a reality that isn't just true in the Bible but one people still face in all sorts of ways every day.

While crafting this book, I sat across from a good friend over coffee describing its outline. He looked up at me with lost eyes and said, "Will you have a chapter on disappointment?" He then rehearsed his story, one I'd watched him live through. In the midst of his fulfilling academic career, a new department chair who didn't like the cut of his jib got him fired before washing out herself. He had only an MFA, which in this PhD-heavy world would never get him hired anywhere. Now, middle-aged, with a mortgage and a passel of kids, he couldn't even think about doctoral work. So she effectively ended his teaching career ... forever. Done. Scorched earth. Move on. What does he do? Believe harder? Or go get a job as a part-time church choir director? He did the latter. Good for him; he made the right choice. But he now struggles with a systemic sense of failure and loss.

Or what of the former student of mine who completed his MA, then his ThM, only to be rejected by every PhD program in his price-geographic range? No one will hire you with *merely* a ThM. End of career. What does he do? Believe harder? Or go get a job in IT? He did the latter. Good for him; he made the right choice. But now he, too, struggles with a sense of failure and loss.

We have to face this. This is what people's lives are actually like. It's what's waiting for you if you've blown up your life. Whatever the way forward is for you, it does not lie in getting it all back.

Whatever you were before—church accountant, teaching pastor, college professor, worship leader, schoolteacher—it's probable that you will never do that work again. One wise pastor, trying to gauge where I was in the healing process, asked me with unexpected directness, "Are you prepared to never preach a sermon again?" The question hurt, but it was actually one of the more penetrating and helpful things he could have asked me, because it addressed my *actual* situation. Who am I without that thing for which I worked so long? How do I live a meaningful life in the face of *that* loss? Of losses I will never get back?

The Wrong Way of Dealing with It

The most common answer I hear is mere horse hockey. And I wish to warn you against a line of false hope being peddled out there, for it will do you serious harm.

Some will offer you the winking promise that if you just

believe hard enough or just claim God's promises, then God will heave to and perform your miracle. But if that miracle doesn't appear, the problem isn't God, it's you—your faulty faith, your persistent doubt, or your shallow spirituality.

My problem with such a proclamation isn't that the quality of one's faith is unimportant, nor even that the statement might be *biblically* false (I tend to think it is). Its great harm is that it's *statistically* false. It's a teaching that ignores and berates the experience of most of the people who hear it.

A person who is incapable or unwilling to "believe harder" may be a "bad Christian" on these terms. Fair enough. But that does not change the fact that they still have to live some sort of Christian life in the throes of their non-miracle. The believe-harder answer does not orient reeling persons like you and me toward the future but toward the past. It tells us to look back over our shoulder to lost glory days with the demand that God bring them back.

When the miracle fails to show up for whatever reason, here's what actually results: My first year of teaching, I had a wheel-chair-bound student who'd lost his ability to walk due to a severed spinal cord in an accident five years prior. He failed my class and left school because instead of completing any of the course requirements and working toward a college degree that might actually help him build a life, he spent night after night at the local healing services trying to "have sufficient faith" to walk again. He was convinced that if only he believed hard enough, God was obliged to knit him a new spinal cord. Then every time it didn't happen, it increased his sense of failure and doubt. So rather than rebuilding a life oriented toward some new goodness, he was trapped in a church-sanctioned atavism that had cost him five years of looking over his shoulder, demanding that, in his words, God "give back what he took."

You might say he misunderstood the teaching, and I might

agree with you. But it's a teaching that persistently encourages such misunderstandings, so I'm warning you against it. The historical facts are plain. For every widow Elijah saved through bottomless jars of flour and oil, dozens starved in the famine. For every blind man Jesus healed at the Pool of Siloam, a score remained unseeing. This may be weak faith; I don't know. But my eyes tell me with certainty that this is how God runs the world. It's a fact. And even facts that hurt are, in the end, our friends.

The hook of the "believe harder" teaching is that it's not absolutely false. It's true *enough* to be compelling till it doesn't work. It's built upon a truth—with God all things *are* possible. Absolutely. If God so wills, God could make me a seminary professor again. I would not mind if God did so. The question is not what God *can* do, but how I am to orient myself toward the sorts of things I am *likely* to face in my journey. By definition, miracles are rare. If they happened to everyone, all the time, they would be not miracles but science.

It's not enough to just believe. Alongside your belief in God's miraculous power, you need a solid understanding of biblical lament. Lament is a sound and godly response to the absent miracle for people like me, mere broken professors of systematic theology who can't seem to muster "sufficient faith."

The real questions to ask ourselves are, *How do I actually live with my situation when the miracle doesn't happen? What does faith look like for persons who must now fight for every scrap of meaning they're likely to find in the world?*

How Shall We Then Live?
The Delicate Dance of Hope and Realism

There's no other way forward for people like you and me. Somehow I must be able to stand before the mirror each morning amid all my shame and sense of failure and realistically and honestly plant myself for that day between Christian lament and Christian hope. The only sane approach is to find a way to both affirm the limitless power of God to overturn my failures in some real and unpredictable way and likewise affirm that for inscrutable reasons, God does not often do so.

There is one exception in the Bible to the uncomfortably persistent pattern of people who screwed up, lost everything, and didn't get it back.

The apostle Peter.

Here we meet both the example and the exception. He blows it. He fails his Master utterly. Thrice a denier and traitor, he runs weeping into the night a broken man. Then his Master is dead, yet even if he weren't, Peter is no good to him now. For all the clarity of his great confession—"You are the Christ, the Son of the Living God"[26]—when push comes to punch, he's a coward.

> The question is not what God can do, but how am I to orient myself toward the sorts of things I am likely to face in my journey.

This is why it doesn't look like the resurrection changes anything for Peter. John looks and believes. Good for him. He followed Jesus to his cross. He is still in good standing. He is still of some use to his Master. But not Peter. Peter looks into the tomb, seems to experience a hesitating belief, and yet his rejoicing is muted.

In fact, John tells us almost as a postscript that Peter went fishing. Why?

Why not?

Jesus is alive, and I'm sure Peter is happy about it. Nothing about his denial changed his love for Jesus. In his heart, he still *wants* to be a disciple. He still *wants* Jesus to be alive. When Jesus shows up at the shore of the sea, it's still Peter who throws himself into the water to get to him first. There's no question of his *desire*.

At issue are his opportunities, his qualifications, his desirability. A risen and victorious Jesus needs faithful Johns, not fickle Peters. While Peter is happy for Jesus, he is of no use to him now. End of his career as a disciple ... forever. Done. Scorched earth. Move on.

So he goes back to fishing. Good for him. He did right. It was the responsible thing for a married man (by my math, a man who has a mother-in-law is married)[27] to get back to work feeding his family. The Jesus years were now part of a past he could romanticize. With eyes full of nostalgia, he could tell his grandchildren about the three-year stint where he got to be part of something special. Something that became great and changed the world. He saw it at the start—he bought Amazon at its initial public offering ... and then sold it a week later for $30 a share while others held on to it and watched it skyrocket. Yes, he would watch the birth of the church and its march all over the Roman Empire—pleased to have played a part, but now watching from the sidelines.

He went back to fishing. Nothing in his behavior or words suggests he thought he would do that kind of work again. On the basis of all the scriptural examples he would have known— Moses, Saul, David, Samson—he was right to think so. He had no power to make his story different in any way. He could not redeem himself.

So he did as he should—began the process of moving on. This is the realist position. Without it, you will not survive the journey that's coming. You will spend all your days mooning over a lost past with its lost potential. You will become bitter and cynical, locked in cycles of "if only"—if only somebody had given me another chance, if only the church hadn't been so cruel or the courts so unfair or the media so predatory. You must embrace whatever is your equivalent of "Jeremy, are you prepared to never preach another sermon?" Answer yes, and get on with living.

And Yet ...

And yet Jesus was not done with Peter. "Feed my sheep."[28] Unique to all the failures and ragamuffins in the whole Bible, Peter is restored—I mean fully restored to the role he had before and more. He goes on to be a rock in the church's foundation, in some sense even *the* rock, chief among the twelve. Still a bit wishy-washy—just ask Paul[29]—but given back a place of greater honor and usefulness than he had before. Even the stigma of it washed away and never mentioned again.

I'd like to promise you that. I'd like someone to promise *me* that. And yet ...

And yet such cases are rare (John Mark's restoration to Paul's labors via Barnabas *might* be a second case).[30] Such futures are possible with God, but God does not often grant such futures. That is the voice of history and the Bible. Peter's story is there to show us what God *can* do, what is within the divine power. It is *not* there to teach me that this *is* the divine will for me ... or for you. It is folly to think otherwise.

Your life may—nay, probably will—consist of a smaller sphere of influence than you had before. You will need to learn contentment and fulfillment in different things and in different ways. I believe they are out there for you—they have been for me. But they will not consist in "getting it all back."

Here again, we learn the lesson of resurrection. The only things that qualify for it are dead things. You must let the past die. Hope and believe that God is powerful enough to do beyond your expectations, yes—we've seen it in Peter—yet don't wait for it. Get busy rebuilding the life you now have. It may feel deficient and inadequate compared to your former life—it probably is. But it is your life now, and it is a gift.

CHAPTER 20

LIVING WITH THE GUILT OF HAVING HURT OTHERS

A new doctor in a psychiatric unit asked the nurse about a young patient who lay unmoving in her bed day after day without speaking.

"Oh, her? Tragic story. She used to be a school bus driver, poor thing. One snowy morning, her bus slid over the edge of an embankment and rolled. Bunch of kids died. Courts never figured out why it happened—faulty brakes, slick road, another driver, maybe all of it—but she hasn't said a word since."

The doctor decided to make it his mission to reach the young woman and spent weeks at her bedside, speaking to her inert form, encouraging her to not blame herself. After all, it might have happened to anyone.

Then one day her lips moved, and she mumbled, "Tell all that to the children."

And he realized he could not ... for they were already dead.

USED TO DO A LOT OF MY SERMON WRITING AT A LOCAL microbrewery. Its second floor was always abandoned on Tuesday nights, and nothing promotes good homiletics like a mindful Hefeweizen in a quiet public house. One night the barkeep walked up to me and said, "I started coming to your church." Turns out she was a recently divorced mother of two, trying to figure out the next chapter of her life. After that, I waved at her at church when I saw her, and our children's pastor told me her kids loved the program. Every few weeks, I'd see her at the pub and ask how she was. I learned that her divorce had been a brutal one and she said my sermons were really helping her heal and move on.

But a few months later, my scandal broke, and the church blew up. I didn't go back to the pub for a long time, but at one point I asked the children's pastor about her. He said, "Oh, her? She hasn't been back in months." That was one of the lowest points of my whole journey.

What are you supposed to do with the knowledge that your choices have destroyed other people? How do you live with the memory of the faces of the people you hurt? What do you do with the powerlessness you feel to fix, redress, or in any way mitigate the damage of your own choices? These questions haunt all of us in one form or another. Everyone has regrets. We've all been hurt by people and have surely hurt others in innumerable ways.

I think leaders, however, bear a special responsibility for the harm they inflict on the people who follow them. It's a special class of sin, less like a starving man stealing a mutton chop and more like a shepherd who eats the sheep in his care. As Plato rightly reminded us in *The Republic*, the only reason leaders exist at all is for the sake of those who follow, so when they do things that destroy those people, it's a uniquely pungent form of evil. If we deny this, then we need to stop reading here and go back to chapter 1, for self-deception of a particularly insidious kind knocks at our door.

The only alternative is to admit the guilt, own it, and deal with the crippling shame that such a confession brings.

From Despair to Gospel

It's a horrible thing to suspect that someone's life may have been better for *not* having met you—someone like that poor young woman at the pub. When I was finally up to going out in public, I eventually went back to that little taproom. She wasn't there. She'd moved on. God alone knows where.

I have died a thousand deaths in my heart over what I did to her. I don't even remember her name, and I wouldn't recognize her now if I passed her on the street. But the thought of her journey—how she was finally beginning to find some hope but had now shrunk back into the shadows, perhaps with deeper wounds than when she met me, perhaps in disgust even leaving the whole church—well, that tears me up. And since I don't really know what happened to her, shame makes me imagine the worst. It wakes me at night in cold sweats. And she is just one of many such stories.

A few people have told me they still remember my time at the church with fondness, that they learned a lot, that they still appreciate things I taught, and I'm grateful when such stories come to me. They help mitigate the sense of absolute failure. But they can't release me from the burden that many hundreds of others may have thrown up their hands and walked away from the church, from God, from their own lives because of me. No, such well-wishers cannot release me. They don't have the power, and I don't have the right to let them. You don't get to weigh the good you've done in life on the scale against the evil and then, if the good outweighs the bad, think well of yourself. That's not how the world works. And it is certainly not how God works.

When confronted with your failures, you don't get to wave your successes in God's face and say, *Look—I have compensated for my sins with my righteous acts.* That is neither Christianity nor the gospel. If I may be blunt, the gospel, at least as the prophet Isaiah forecasts it, says if I am attempting to clothe myself in even my most righteous actions, they will be revealed to have only the value of used menstrual rags. Yes, that's literally what Isaiah said.[31] Who would wrap themselves in those, stand before the mirror, and say, "See my fancy new clothes?" The naked emperor in all his pompous self-deception was better off than that.

No, the gospel of Jesus Christ never weighs our good actions against our evil ones and then takes a sum. The stains of our sin are not removed by any amount of countervailing good. We do not diligently darn our bloody rags into wedding gowns. As Aslan said to the dragonish Eustace after his repeated attempts to shed his scaly skin, "You will have to let me undress you."[32] Our rags must be shed, and we must be dressed in another's clothes—in another's righteousness.

How Shall We Then Live?
Embrace the Oldest Truth Once Again

This is an old truth, one of the oldest, and if you're reading this because you were once in a position to proclaim that truth, then you already know it well. I am reminding you that the message you once proclaimed to others applies to you still. You cannot remit, remove, or reduce your agonized conscience by any subsequent act of virtue. Nor can such a conscience be answered by anyone sincerely reminding you of the good you did once upon a time. Be grateful for such reminders, but do not rest your heart upon them. They are not strong enough to silence for long a disturbed and voluble conscience.

Learn again that first lesson of the faith, my friend. Our sins cannot be outlived or outlasted; they can only be forgiven. And there is only one who has the power to answer the recriminations of our heart. St. John reminds us that when our own heart condemns us, God is greater than our heart.[33] There it is. That same Christ you spent all that time pointing people toward now beckons to you to come again and find rest in the only place it is to be found.

I can't undo whatever I did to that poor young lady at the brewing company or a hundred others just like her. I cannot make it right. It's beyond my power. I must live with it. I can only go to Jesus, offering my remorse and shame as the only offering I have to bring, believing in faith that *he* has not lost track of her or anyone else. That he has the power to redeem even where I destroyed. He has done it for Adam's folly, and he can do it for yours and mine. He bids me to lay *this* burden down as he bids us to do with all others and let him carry it.

> Our sins cannot be outlived or outlasted; they can only be forgiven.

This does not in any way make me less responsible for the things I did and the hurts I caused. It means only that those who are now lost to me are not lost to God, and I have to rest in that. That is what faith looks like. You once gave your own life to Christ? Perhaps it's time to entrust him with all those other people's lives as well.

CHAPTER 21

LIVING WITH THE UNEXPECTED CONSEQUENCES

The doctor was frustrated. After completing the physical on the morbidly obese man, he could not understand the man's ongoing shock and disbelief.

"Sir, you've been eating poorly for years, against my advice. You know that, right?"

"Yes."

"Then you had to have known there'd be consequences eventually, right?"

"Yes."

"Diabetes?"

"Yes."

"Respiratory trouble?"

"Yes."

"Joint pain?"

"Yes."

"High blood pressure?"

"Yes."

"Then I don't understand why you're so surprised at your condition?"

"Well, I wasn't expecting to get so fat."

YOU GET TO PICK YOUR CHOICES. YOU DON'T GET TO PICK your consequences. I've said this before, but now that life is settling down for you, you may start seeing the truth of it with new eyes. You're probably becoming aware of some unexpected consequences you might not have noticed before. I remember the slowly growing realization that some things in my life were just never going to bounce back to what they were. The brokenness I would carry with me was of a much broader and more enduring kind. Have you yet noticed that different sorts of consequences invite difference sorts of responses from us? Let me explain.

Natural consequences. These are the most obvious. The universe is so arranged that if you jump off the roof, the broken leg is the natural result. It's entailed within the definition of the choice. I've talked about the natural consequences of my choices before—the loss of my positions at the church and seminary, the social stigma that comes with being "a failed pastor." These sorts of consequences hurt, yes, but they don't tend to cause soulish rancor, except temporarily the way the broken leg does. Such things you come to terms with at a reasonable pace and move on, because in a sense, you expected them.

Even the legal proceedings and criminal record were the natural result of my having broken the law the way I did. I don't mean they were absolutely necessary. Lorelai might have chosen not to lean into the charges. That she did, however, was her right. So again, since it was predictable, coming to terms with it was painful, but what could I say? I did the thing, and this was the result. Eventually, you just have to shrug and move on.

Un-natural consequences. On the other hand, I've mentioned other consequences that seemed gratuitous, that felt like a pile-on—the media treatment, for example, or the brutal manner in which the university prosecuted my termination. These felt very different to me.

You may disagree. You may say these, too, were part of the deal. You may say these were natural, just unexpected. That's fair. We are most likely to label "unfair" those things that come upon us unexpectedly. I won't quibble the point.

But it opens a Pandora's lunchbox of questions. We expected that jumping off the roof might break our leg. But what if we discovered six months later that this jump had somehow also given us diabetes? The thread of natural causality might be just as strong, but the diabetes *feels* very different from the fractured tibia. It *seems* unrelated. It would be understandable if we spat a bit more venom at the universe over the never-ending insulin shots than over the plaster cast. Whether or not we call them *unfair*, we still have the question of how we live with such consequences.

The Body Remembers–
A Series of Unexpected Losses

I imagine by now you've begun to realize that the losses have touched places of your life you didn't think were even related to it. I wonder if any of yours overlap with mine.

Cognitively. For one, almost overnight I lost my ability to memorize—and not merely in the sense that aging always slows this function. At forty, I was still memorizing whole books of the Bible. Two years later, I couldn't remember a grocery list of three items. Denise noticed it on her own, with no small amount of frustration. Also, I somehow lost much of my capacity to self-motivate and manage the details of my life. A permanent sort of white noise exists inside my head that gets in the way whenever I try to focus on theological material. I just can't think with the same academic clarity as before. I've since learned that depression changes brain chemistry. Apparently, I volunteered to be the poster child for the phenomenon.

Was this a *natural* consequence? I don't know. It was certainly unexpected. The gift just went away, like Samson's strength. I can't find a direct relationship between those painful events and my loss of executive function, nor can I find another cause.

I could go on in this vein for some time—a loss of social confidence, a loss of sense of wellbeing, a loss of determination and assertiveness, a general loss of hardiness of life.

Physically. The severe and rapid weight loss I experienced during the depression left unexpected marks on my body as well. I won't get into details because … well, I'm not old enough yet to enjoy telling strangers about how "the bile drips, drips, drips day and night." Suffice it to say that in the intervening years, I've had to employ the services of a dermatologist, urologist, ENT, and physical medicine doctor—each of whom has said it's unusual for a person my age to be struggling with these issues. Also, around the time I was making my public confession at the church, my children discovered that about ten percent of the hairs on my reliably lush brown head had gone suddenly gray.

Spiritually. Yes, I've seen spiritual changes as well. For example, I now find singing in church an almost unendurable act. I've a more liturgical bent, so my relationship with the praise and worship movement has always been a bit tentative, but now I'm almost impervious to popular Christian music—especially when played by a band on a Sunday morning.

This one I think I can trace a bit more directly. During the year of my entanglement with Lorelai, I did in fact dive into the emotional fervor of contemporary worship with vim. I think that was partly because I thought it was important for a congregation to "see a pastor worship"—a deficient but understandable motive. The bigger reason for my Vineyard period was that I was in spiritual hell and seeking a way out. To stand there on Sunday with my hands raised and tears running down my face was a way of pouring out my grief as well as a way of pleading with God for help.

I think it was the public equivalent to what happened on my living room floor every night at 2:00 a.m., when I would wallow and weep, moaning out my Augustinian prayer, "Dear God, save me from this ... only not quite yet."

I think those months of anguish so tightly bonded with the sound and feel of contemporary praise choruses that even now I can't stand to hear them without wanting to sigh and sit down—and I often do. Something about my journey took from me my capacity to enter into such music, even with teenagers who love it! And the distance this creates between us, I grieve.

What About Your Losses?

What about *your* equivalent losses—physical, emotional, spiritual? Losses that, while clearly caused by or related to all that trouble, are also disconnected from it, like the universe piling on stuff needlessly. What are you and I to do with these hellish gifts?

Honestly, the only perspective I've found helpful is to recognize that most everything you could list—losses in economics, health, relationships, physical skills—were all going to happen anyway. Life is a terminal disease. Nobody gets out alive.

Whatever virtue people gain as they age in order to face with dignity the declines of body and mind, you have self-selected to learn on an advanced timetable.

> Whatever virtue people gain as they age in order to face with dignity the declines of body and mind, you have self-selected to learn on an advanced timetable.

Did your marriage fail? Well, all marriages end eventually. It's why we have the word *widow*. Did your health break? Well, visit a nursing home and look around. Did you lose your employability or livelihood or your dignity?

Well, visit a few war veterans. Your home? Visit some refugees. Your public reputation? Well, consider yourself blessed. You won't be asked to go into politics.

Don't you see? You have no choice but to take a stoic view of such losses, because they were coming for you anyway, just in different clothing and on a different timetable.

The question cannot be how you get them back but rather what sort of meaningful life you will build within these new realities. If we learn anything from reading human history, it is that we are resilient creatures. Most everything that exists of any historical beauty or worth—from cathedrals to djembes, from oil portraits to spicy cuisine—was created by suffering people who created it anyway in the midst of their disadvantage and want.

How Shall We Then Live? A Suggestion

One way I've found to remind myself of how blessed I am even amid the unexpected reductions and limitations is to do some reading in history. Perhaps a classic like Barbara Tuchman's *The Distant Mirror: The Calamitous 14th Century* or, frankly, anything by a real historian. I promise you that by the time you work your imagination through the Black Plague, the Papal Schism, the Hundred Years' War, and roving bands of pillaging brigands, you will look upon your cellular, air-conditioned, power-steering, on-demand, cotton-poly life as extraordinarily blessed.

If this feels like a mere therapeutic strategy, congratulations, you broke the code. As a therapist once admitted to me, "I spend much of my time just helping people find an interpretation of their tragedy they can live with." Yes, because live with them we must.

Much of your journey now will consist not of dramatic and inspiring successes but of fighting small daily battles with your mind, body, and spirit. Mundane battles where the victories often depend on such tiny things as what you choose to eat; whether you get sufficient rest, exercise, or sunlight; and what internal monologues you allow yourself to entertain. They are not the lesser part of the Christian walk for being measly or monotonous. They make up the bulk of human life, and the shape of your soul going forward greatly depends on whether such skirmishes are won or lost.

I think you'll be surprised at the meetings you'll have with God over "nonspiritual" issues like memory, insomnia, cholesterol, back pain, and loneliness if only you're willing to lift them up in a spirit of sincere offering. God is very good at using physical pain to do spiritual good—even when the pain is a consequence of our own action.

CHAPTER 22

THE WAY OF REPENTANCE
AND FORGIVENESS

The negotiator tried his best to hide his frustration. Neither representative from either side of the civil war had given an inch at any stage of the peace talks. It was a tragedy all around. Both sides had employed a scorched-earth method of war. Thousands were dead. The prosperity of the nation wasted.

Now finally at the table, neither would concede anything—not on territory, not on arms usage, not even on the shape of the negotiation table. The arbitrator put his head in his hands. Surely, there had to be something they could agree on.

Then it hit him. One side or the other had fired the first shot. That at least was a historical fact. Maybe someone would at least own that.

"Oh, that's easy," said the first.

"I agree!" said the second. "That's obvious."

"Well, then," said the negotiator hopefully, "whose fault is this war?"

Each pointed at the other and shouted, "Theirs!"

And he realized that by now they were both right.

ONE OF THE MOST FREQUENT AND HARDEST THINGS I heard people say after I blew up my life was, "He doesn't seem very sorry for what he did." At the same time, one of the more difficult things my wife wrestled with was, Why does it take so long for people to forgive? If they can't forgive now, why can they in six months? What difference does time make? Her perspective had never occurred to me. I was consumed with feelings of relief at having my mind and family back, and ... well, a little anger, too, over all the unexpected consequences. In hindsight, I understand why I didn't look penitent, and you can't expect people to extend forgiveness to the impenitent, can you?

Forgiveness? Repentance? What are we to do with them?

I could point you to a dozen books on the nature of forgiveness, fewer on the nature of repentance. Yet the two are supposed to work together. As a start, let's imagine what might be an ideal situation. Some evil has been done, something small like a white lie or something worse like a betrayal of friendship or marriage. Whatever happened and however it came about, the peace between you and someone else has been breached. What is supposed to happen is that the offender owns the wrong they've done and repents of it, and the offended party receives that confession and forgives. From here, the relationship is restored, now stronger for having endured a hard journey. Or, at the very least, it has found a new footing on which to grow.

The ideal, however, seldom happens. It can break down at any step. The offender may never know they've done harm, or perhaps they never intended it, or perhaps they're truly unrepentant of it. Or they may no longer be around due to incarceration, relocation, or death. On the other hand, the offended party may refuse to forgive or may nurse a desire for vengeance. And of course, even this assumes nice clean lines between offender and offended. More often, while one party may commit the initial and obvious offense, by the time all the recriminations are over and the full history is known, both parties often need to extend and receive forgiveness. And then this troubling question: Are some things unforgivable, harms so great that even if these steps are taken reconciliation never really happens? This is an impossibly complicated issue, but I've learned a few important things about it that you should know for navigating them in your own story.

Defining Terms

While there are lots of profitable ways to define these terms, I take the center of *repentance* to be the recognition of the harm my actions have caused you and the taking of responsibility for it. That is, I own what I did, knowing it to have been an evil. And the center of *forgiveness* I take to be your releasing me from further debt and recriminations. And the word *further* here is important, because repentance and forgiveness do not mitigate just consequences. I may repent, and you may forgive, and yet I may still have to endure the legal and natural consequences of my actions. Forgiveness means the releasing of your desire to hold the act against me indefinitely. It allows me, the offender, to "do my time," "pay my societal debt," or however you wish to say it, and then experience restoration. And finally, *reconciliation*, which hopefully follows out of all this justice, consists of the restoring of normalized relations between the two of us. And while repentance and forgiveness don't always produce reconciliation, real reconciliation can't happen without them.

> Forgiveness can be given even before repentance has occurred.

Forgiveness and Repentance:
Brothers Under the Skin

One surprising thing I've learned is just how much alike repentance and forgiveness are, even though they are usually considered opposites.

First, both repentance and forgiveness require a choice. Neither happens accidently or against your will. You can't simply wait long enough and have them appear. My wife was right. No amount of mere time will make us either remorseful or magnanimous. Either party can be stubborn indefinitely. And neither is an easy choice. Both parties must release something in the bargain. To admit you were wrong will cost you your pride, and to forgive, you must lay aside your desire for recrimination.

Second, who should go first? Repentance certainly comes first logically. Forgiveness can often be more robust when it's responding to an admission of wrong by the other. But the truth is, neither need wait for the other.

Yes, I am suggesting that forgiveness can be given even before repentance has occurred. I believe this because it is the model of our Lord. St. Paul said, "While we were still sinners, Christ died for us."[34] In this, forgiveness shows off its "eternal" quality, for God has in some real sense forgiven us in eternity, then also forgiven us temporally in the death and resurrection of Christ. Further, we experience this forgiveness in the moment of our conversion, and it is fully enacted in us only in our final redemption one day. God's forgiveness, while nonnegotiably bound up with our repentance, is not held hostage to it.

So I do not believe forgiveness must wait for repentance, nor that repentance must wait for forgiveness. They belong together, but where one party refuses to play their role, we must yet faithfully play our own.

Third, it can, however, be difficult to tell when the other party really has done their part. This is because neither repentance nor forgiveness has a single mode of expression. You cannot measure the depth or sincerity of either by any metric of the moment. Every immediate indicator—tears, emotional fervor, use of specific words—can be fabricated intentionally or accidently, as when children figure out that they can say both "I'm sorry" and "I forgive you" when they really aren't and don't. Adults are equally adept at this game.

Further, real repentance or forgiveness truly may have happened where none of the expected signs appear. I love the line in the fourth *Harry Potter* book, where after a long feud between Harry and his best friend, Ron, it reads, "Harry knew that Ron was about to apologize and suddenly he found he didn't need to hear it."[35] It's a trope found often in literature that men can be reconciled without words, whereas women cannot be reconciled without tears. This is perhaps unfair to both sexes (I'm weepier than Denise is by far), but it does illustrate the point. We must not put preconditions on how repentance or forgiveness are externally clothed. True repentance may or may not be accompanied by tears and groanings. And real forgiveness may be granted where no words are even exchanged.

How, then, are we to know whether someone really has repented or truly forgiven?

To answer that, fourth, we must realize that both are a journey, not an event. We seldom enact them perfectly the first time we try. He who repents of wrong is probably only partially aware of the pain his actions have caused. Thus there will be a growth in the nature and quality of the repentance, and new things may need to be repented of as that clarity grows.

I was always struck by the fact that the very people in history who seemed most aware of and broken by their sins were the great saints, those whom you would think had the least to repent of. But they knew something we don't. When you contemplate the depth of our offense against God or others—it's true of both—we may find forgiveness, yes, but we also discover with agonizing clarity that our sins were more heinous, more hurtful, more destructive than we initially thought. Repentance is not a single act to be gotten over with and then shoved into the past. It's a way of being human, and if done properly, will teach us to loathe evil and sin sufficiently that we cease from doing it in future.

Finally and most ominously, neither repentance nor forgiveness is optional. It is the clear testimony of the Scriptures that the result of refusing either one is damnation. He who will not repent shall not see God. He who refuses to forgive the trespasses of others shall not have his own forgiven. It is the harshest of messages, but it's clear to me now that when we refuse to repent of the evil we do or determinedly resist releasing others from their debts, hell is precisely the word for what we are choosing. We shut ourselves up in a new cycle of self-deception or hate, both of which are deadly to the soul and can have only one destination. We must recall both words of our Lord—"Repent and believe"and "Forgive as you have been forgiven."[36]

Your Ongoing Journey of Repentance

So far this has been a somewhat theoretical exhortation on repentance and forgiveness, but now we must bring these truths to bear on our situation. What does it mean for people who've done wrong—for perpetrators of evil like you and me—to lean into this reality?

Repentance is obviously the first conversation we must have. By this stage of your journey, you've probably had several—possibly conflicting—sorts of experience with repentance. What does real repentance look like? How do we know when we've "felt" it sufficiently? Honestly, I can't answer that question. I can only record my journey with it, and perhaps it will resonate with you.

I remember several distinct stages of coming to terms with what I had done. The first was an immediate overwhelming horror over what I had made myself into, barely distinguishable from pride. *I always thought I was better than that. People of my pedigree don't do such things.* Deficient, yes, but very real.

As the life-destroying consequences began to reveal themselves, I experienced a sorrow that was equal parts repentance and mere embarrassment over "getting caught."

Two months in, the faces of the "dead and wounded" began to swim before my eyes, and another wave of nausea-like repentance sent me on a tour of meetings with elders, congregants, and former colleagues, making personal apologies for having made their lives hell. I met with every possible response from a nonplussed "Oh, we weren't really that hurt" to the angry "I don't want to meet with you." In several cases, these moments jumpstarted reconciliation between me and the other person. In others, it set the breach in cement.

Two months after that, while reading the penitential psalms, I was flung despairingly into bed for three days in horror and grief over my betrayal of my office, the gospel, and Christ.

At the eight-month mark, as I made my public confession before the church, I felt simply numb. I was sorry, yes, but the political hypocrisy it entailed by so many left the repentance a tight abstract intellectual reality I could articulate in clear and concise words but had no real feeling about.

Five years later, when I was invited back to that same elder group to "try again," all I had left was a long litany of regrets—*I wish I had done this and that differently. I regret not doing this or that.*

At the nine-year mark, I was confronted with the subtle and cancerous consequences in my own children's spiritual lives that only began to surface at that time. I was broken with a new and exquisite horror as I watched the weight of my own folly borne by my kids now as life-defining trauma. Dear God, not this too!

Which one of the above penitential stages reflected the *real* moment of repentance? You must see that it's the wrong question. They were all real. Repentance is not the act of a moment, like dropping a ball. No, it seems to bounce back into your hand in a repeating cycle of mortification. It's a process that will take your whole life. And each time it comes back to you, you must make the disciplined choice again.

So don't run from such moments. Lean in and realize that God is busy in all of them. Repentance is not a stage from which you emerge but a companion who walks with you all along the way.

Forgiveness: The Great Temptation

If you're a "casual" reader of this book, you may wonder why a section on forgiveness would even be necessary. After all, I'm writing to the perp—the one *needing* forgiveness. Isn't it misguided to suggest that the one who caused all the grief needs to forgive something? If, however, you are the one I'm writing to—the one who shipwrecked your own life—you know exactly why this section is needed.

Yes, it's true that I have much for which I need to be forgiven, but only in a court of law are clean black-and-white lines between perpetrator and victim preserved. Real life is often much grayer. Usually by the time a life has come apart fully, a lot of hurt has been passed around.

But it is correct to observe the inherent danger in this discussion for us. The admission that we may have to forgive someone implies that we, too, have been wronged in some way. That means someone else bears some measure of guilt in this story. The temptation, then, is to seize the fact that you are not the *only* blameworthy person. An unhealthy desire might grow here to spread some of that guilt around, to diffuse it, as in, *Here's my opportunity to limit my own culpability.*

That is what we must *not* do. Somehow, by some impossible measure of grace, we must learn to think about the wrongs done to us, but without it becoming a means by which we dodge our own responsibility for the wrongs we did.

I know the danger well. How much time did I spend raging around my empty living room over the fact that Lorelai's role was never told? She never owned her share of the guilt—on the monstrously sophistical grounds that I broke the law before it was all discovered. I seethed at the college administration for not giving me a hearing and at the church elders for ... well, not hearing me at all. I steamed and stormed at the media, imagining, like a little child sent to his room without supper, how they would report my death if all the public shaming sent my motorcycle into an overpass abutment at 80 mph. Oh, how I boiled and bristled each time I got a crank call or received a cancellation email for a speaking engagement. And most of all, I spluttered forth my imprecations at the church and a society that told me at every turn that my grief was illegitimate and without merit, a church and society interested only in whether I could produce on command bitter, salty tears of remorse.

So you realize why, while standing in *that* space, it would've been folly for someone to talk to me about a need for me to forgive wrongs done to me. It would have only poured kerosene on my heart's blaze and confirmed that I was right to inwardly burn. But by now you and I have walked many pages together, and I hope we understand ourselves better. So here near the end of the book, I will risk talking about forgiveness. Perhaps it is time.

Our Unique Journey: Why Even We Must Forgive

It becomes complicated when, as is often the case, the lines between perpetrator and victim grow blurry. Lots of permutations exist here as well. Lorelai and I were coconspirators, but for a variety of reasons, the blame fell on me. The church and university were all innocent parties—true victims, if you will. And yet in the process of grappling with the consequences of my actions, they made many choices that increased my and my family's agonies. These were decisions made in response to mine, as if I had thrown the first big rock into the lake, creating great and horrible waves. But then many others hurled their own rocks till the lake was a roiling and churning deep where everyone was drenched.

Who outside of the omniscient Judge of heaven could possibly sort out the allotments of guilt owned by each party? I certainly have abandoned any attempt to do so in my own story, and you must do the same in yours. This is not an exercise in assigning blame; it is an exercise in granting forgiveness.

The threshold of responsibility for forgiveness is disturbingly low—a mere acknowledgment of pain given, grief caused, wrong done. It need not belabor, draw up lists, or memorialize those wrongs. It must only be able to call them what they were—evils.

The reason you must forgive is not so you may have additional fortifications for your anger and bitterness but so you may release them. The discipline of forgiving others forms us into the kind people who are less likely to do wrong to others. I maintain that if the worst tyrants in history—the Hitlers, the Stalins, the Khans—had practiced the discipline of forgiving the small wrongs done to them in life, they would have by that art learned to not be tyrants.

Whether your grievances are legitimate or not makes no difference. Whether others concede them as legitimate or not is irrelevant. You must learn to forgive even *perceived* grievances because even wholly imaginary ones, left unaddressed, grow gangrenous with time. They will rot your soul with the same surety as the indisputable grievance. Forgiveness cares not whether courts, administrators, or peers think your beef is legitimate. If your heart rears up on its hind legs over what someone has done to you, then your only safe path forward is the one that travels through the realm of forgiveness.

How Shall We Then Live: Learning to Forgive

All forgiveness is hard, and you'll need a holier guide than me on the general process. But I have a few specific comments on the unique situation of the perpetrator of evil who also has some forgiving to do.

First, you will probably never be able to confront the person who caused you pain, and more, you will probably never hear repentance from them. This is just a fact of the context. When the church elders were confronted by others over how they prosecuted my case, their response was a halfhearted, "We're sorry if anything we did was painful, but we did right. It's what we had to do." You should prepare yourself for this *sorry-not-sorry* sort of response. You may be able to judge your progress in forgiving by how sympathetically you can hear such a statement. Can you accept that they honestly believe it, that they are not merely shaming or hiding but truly have clear consciences about their actions? It's very possible they do.

Second, give yourself time. Just as our sense of remorse waxes and wanes over time, in and out of season, so does our capacity to forgive. I have days when I hardly think at all about those past events or people. Then I'll pass the university on the way to the store—or worse, pass the house where it all went down with its new owners out in the driveway playing basketball—and my innards will double-clutch and grind, and it'll feel like that first month all over again.

Third, continue to strive for an honest balance between your own guilt and that of others. It's understandable that some days your own sins will weigh more, and on other days, hurts you've endured will be the heavier. That's to be expected and not a sign of failure.

Finally, a caveat. We must never underestimate the power of the gospel to reconcile even the worst enemies. I write these words less than a decade after the events. I know much will change in me and in others over the next decade and beyond. I have heard stories of broken marriages restored—mine was. I have heard stories of broken people returning to pastoral ministry or other professions. I have heard stories of greater evils than yours and mine overturned by the power of the cross. I cannot promise you will experience that level of reconciliation, but we must not preclude it either. Such things are possible even if they are uncommon. Do not forget, God the Father has made sons and daughters out of the very people who murdered his Son. That is ultimately the bar against which our efforts are judged.

CHAPTER 23

THE TYRANNY OF
ABSOLUTE COMMITMENT

The career missionary was wrapping up his final sermon of Revival Week in the Sowers Bible College chapel. It had been a remarkable set of meetings with the whole student body. Now it all came down to this moment—the final plea.

"And if you're willing to promise to God that, if God so wills, you'll become a foreign missionary to whatever part of the world needs you most, get out of that seat and walk down the aisle. Make your commitment public!"

Instantly, two hundred students were on their feet, streaming down the aisle as tears streamed down their faces.

Yes, it had been a remarkable week.

A week every one of those two hundred students would remember the rest of their lives.

A week that in twenty years would drive 197 of them into therapy to deal with the shame of having broken their promise.

T HE DIFFICULT THING ABOUT DISCUSSING THE FUTURE IS that, without fail, you end up talking about the past. This is so because much of our future is determined by what we did in our past but also because the future inevitably—and far too quickly—becomes the past. Past, present, future—they just won't stay put.

Part of your journey forward will be to figure out how to think about the future. While that question is certainly filled with pragmatics like career, family, housing—things I'm not qualified to help you with—you're also going to be wrestling with what it means for you spiritually. What is your future with God? What does God want from you now? This I do have some experience with.

If you were once a servant of the church either clerically, professionally, or as a volunteer, you probably became one because of some internal commitment, some sense of "calling." You probably had a moment or two in your past that confirmed that call, and in light of that, you made all sorts of promises about your future service to God—your "whole life," "whole heart," or something equally universal. Of course you did; it's the first and greatest commandment—to love God with your whole "everything." No one would even consider assuming the many burdens of ministry unless they intended to "give it all."

I'll bet you all the money in my wallet that you now look back on those intentions and commitments with some chagrin. Having now blown it, what now becomes of those promises? What power should those past commitments hold over your future? Should you be making new promises about what you intend to do now?

Intention's Dirty Little Secret

The problem with every promise about the future is that you can't actually *do* anything with the future. All human action takes place in the present. Our relation to the future is, at best, one of *intention*. That is, we can declare intentions today about something we plan to do in the future. These intentions take the form of either promises or preparatory actions—both of which are done now, in the present. We can't actually *do* anything in or to the future itself. It is, from a human perspective, nonexistent.

You can't fish with the rod you *intend* to buy tomorrow. You can't eat the cake you *intend* to bake next week. The only thing you can do with the resources you hope to possess in the future is to form intentions about them. And your ability to anticipate your future resources is limited.

Consider the situation you are now in. Could you have predicted a year ago that you would be here? Ten years ago? I couldn't. When my year-long implosion came, it flowed out of no preexisting material I could have foreseen as a teenager or young adult. My slow-motion tumble stood in contradiction to every *intention* I had ever consciously formed in my life. So much so that no one else in my life expected it either.

That is the problem with intention. It doesn't guarantee a particular result. New material can arrive in your story that can blitz out your most sincere intentions.

Does this mean we should never *intend* anything? That's hardly reasonable. Very little good will flow from us if we do not first intend to do it. But there is a heavy danger in it. If we expect more from an intention than it can give—if we hold unreasonable intentions—we are setting ourselves up for failure in our future.

You are now feeling the failure of whatever promises you made earlier in life. You will be tempted to begin making such promises again, and I want you to think carefully before you do.

The Demand for the Absolute Intention

In my experience, the thing people most often ask us to promise God regarding our future is, well ... *everything*. It's the bread-and-butter center of every revival sermon ever preached—the demand for an absolute commitment to God, a giving of all, your whole future, every minute.

Of course God deserves my all, my whole future, my every

minute. That's not the issue, but a moment's pause will remind us such a promise can really only mean that I *intend* to be as faithful in every future moment as I desire to be at this moment.

Forming such an intention may be a good thing, but it comes with a danger—one you have now discovered. It's one I only discovered after the fact—too late to be useful. During my emotional unraveling, I realized that from my earliest memories, I had been fed a steady diet of total commitment. You owe God your everything, no turning back, no turning back. It came in a hundred different ways—calls to the mission field in college chapels, throw-your-stick-into-the-fire moments at camp, invitations to re-re-rededicate your life in church. Hymns like "I Surrender All" proclaimed its virtues—"*All* to Jesus I surrender"—while the Christian pop music of the day laid the weight of future generations on my eighteen-year-old shoulders, telling me that all who come after us better *Find Us Faithful.*[37]

As I came to understand it, the greatest possible sin, therefore, had to be inconstancy—putting your hand to the plow, then looking back. The greatest failure was the one named by the apostle in the Revelation—being *lukewarm* and consequently *spewed out.* This narrative of absolute commitment was compelling to me. And it played a central role in my downfall.

In response to that call, I lived a chaste and docile life when compared to my contemporaries whom I would occasionally discover making out in locker rooms. I didn't "smoke, or chew, or go with girls that do." Didn't listen to the devil-music. Never snuck out of my house at night to sow wild oats or cast three sheets to the wind. Never did anything that would prevent me from being considered for the Supreme Court or get me kicked out of a governorship. I was happily, contentedly a lifer—a married ascetic with big plans of "being used by God to change the world." So far, so good. My intentions for an absolute commitment made at church altars and summer campfire pits were working out beautifully.

The idea there might be situations in life that could cause me to question this view—that the feelings might ebb or be challenged by a more hedonistic lifestyle—never entered my head. Till I met Lorelai. Throughout this book, I've explained how the attraction of her libidinous life brought all the stated intentions of my youth crashing down, grinding the ascetic's commitment into the dust, making it seem shallow, inauthentic, and unsatisfying. In the end I found myself guilty of the great sin I'd heard about all my life—inconstancy. I had become lukewarm and received the predicted expulsion.

The point: Those absolute commitments of my youth ended up becoming a new source of shame when they didn't work out as I intended. You're probably having a similar realization about your own youthful intentions for your future. The temptation may now be to make renewed absolute commitments. Should you?

Not for my money. I'd like to suggest a better, humbler, more realistic way forward.

How Shall We Then Live? A Better Way

The question cannot be, *How do I make a commitment to God about my future that will stick this time?* It's a bad question that will set you up for more failure. The right question is, *How do I exercise good stewardship over the only thing that's actually in my possession? How do I offer to God, not my* all, *but what I actually possess?*

Of course, that begs the question, *What do I actually possess?*

By way of answer, I refer you to a holier man than I—Brother Lawrence. This post-Reformation French Carmelite monk gave us the reflections that became the classic *The Practice of the Presence of God.*

Brother Lawrence found himself languishing over the dirty dishes in the monastery kitchen when he much rather would have been engaged in the sexier aspects of monastic life—a metaphor for which I suppose I should ask his forgiveness. One of the main things these spiritually dry, physically damp labors taught him was the necessity of finding God in the present rather than in some future pious activity or some longed-for opportunity. I can no longer distinguish whether what I now offer are his conclusions or my own inspired by him. If you'd like to sort that out, go get a copy of his book and read it.

The book metaphorically saved my life and literally saved my sanity as I found myself ousted from a robust public life of service, thrust down into the isolated domesticity of the forgotten homemaker—changing my son's diapers, washing dishes, vacuuming, doing laundry—dreaming of how I would give God a better *everything* if I ever got the chance.

Thanks to Brother Lawrence, I began to realize that this intention of offering to God this impossible future *all* looked suspiciously like the same *all* from my younger days. But Brother Lawrence argued that I should offer God nothing more than my *present*. That is the gift, the only gift, I can actually give. Practically, this meant I was to offer as a gift to God the contents of whatever square of the board I happened to be standing in at present.

Are you worried about the future? Then your required offering to God is not the *future*, over which you have little control, but the *worry* that now consumes you. Are you despairing over your lack of future opportunities? Your required offering is not *the future opportunities*, whatever that means, but the *despair* you presently feel. Do you feel anger? That is your offering. Shame? Then that is your offering. Bitterness or joy, lust or contentment, weakness or vigor—it matters not. God desires the offering you have. The only offering God hates, we're told throughout the Psalms and the Prophets, is the false one—the one that presumes to offer something other than what we possess, the one that tries to offer pious feelings where only dry sorrows dwell. God knows how to receive and glorify lament, brokenness, and weakness, but nothing in heaven or earth can make worthy the insincere offering of the hypocrite. No, better to make a sincere offering of our hypocrisy itself than pretend to offer piety where only doubt dwells. Even the IRS requires you to pay taxes only on your actual wages, not those you intend to make ten years from now.

If you're feeling an urge to make a commitment to God in light of your past failings, well and good. Just make it something you can actually give. Offer God whatever is in your hand right now—bitterness, dissolution, ill-humor, whatever it is. There will be opportunity enough to make offerings about the future. But the moment to make them will be when those futures have rolled into your hand as the present. *Then* you can offer them to God much more profitably and sincerely.

> Offer to God whatever is in your hand right now–bitterness, dissolution, ill-humor, whatever it is.

You and I and Brother Lawrence and Cain himself have the present—only the present. Live in it. God alone holds the past and the future. So let go of them. If you want to have anything to do with them, it will have to be in the present—in your *now*. Your only concern is the square you're standing in. Whether it contains belief or doubt, bitterness or contentment, solace or silence, life or death is ultimately of no concern. The only intention that matters is your intention to make of it an offering to the God who stands in the square with you.

Don't fret that such an offering—sorrow, loss, worry—seems deficient. It certainly is, but offer it anyway. Always offer what you have. God is very good at turning deficient offerings into holiness. God has probably never had any other kind of offering to work with.

CHAPTER 24

THE ~~UN~~CHANGEABLE PAST

It was done. The departed canine companion of so many years was interred with flowers. She tried to feel some sadness for her husband's loss—it had been his dog, after all—but in her heart she was rather glad the mutt was gone. It'd been one of those animals that was impossible to train, always into mischief. Like the time it had stolen and buried her phone, or the time ...

Oh, no matter. She wanted to support her husband, at least till he shuddered and mumbled over the mound of earth, "Goodbye, old friend. You were a good dog."

This was more than she could bear. "Are you kidding me? You griped about him constantly! Remember the messes, the chewed furniture, the holes in the yard. The neighbors were always complaining. You threatened to sell him every other week! I mean, what about the—"

"Yes, yes, he was such a good dog."

T HE MOST SURPRISING FEEDBACK I GOT FROM PEOPLE WHO vetted early versions of this book was that it was "brave" or "honest." This shocked and sobered me. That is actually the opposite of what I felt this book was. Yes, I intended *honest* insofar as I tried not to lie, but in no meaningful sense did I feel it *brave*.

It's an inescapable aspect of our humanity that no one is ever very honest or brave when speaking of their own failures and weaknesses. By this stage of my journey, I've listened to lots of people talk about their own self-inflicted tragedies. I'm surprised how often I think, *They're hiding something. This can't be the whole truth.* I, of all people, thinking another broken person isn't being completely candid? What hypocrisy. What arrogance. You may have thought the same at various points of my story. I don't blame you. I'm not sure we can help it. Short of the divine perspective, there are no full and final tellings of any of our stories—certainly not from our own lips.

No, you don't have in these pages a brave or honest retelling of these events. You have the version I could bear to tell. I don't know if I could articulate the *full* truth—even if I knew it. I don't have the words. This more astringent version of events flows not from a desire to deceive but from a desire not to feel shame.

> We tell our stories, not as they happened, but as we can stand to have them told.

I know what you cannot. I know how all this *really* felt. I know what I was *really* thinking. I know what I *really* wanted at any given moment and would have *really* done if given the chance. Such truth is always much darker, grislier, and more heinous than we can bear to admit in words. Think hard about your own attempts to tell your story to others. How much do you leave out? How many ways do you subtly reframe your motives or thoughts? Surely, you know that little heart-pang that stabs as you speak, *If I said it as I actually felt it, they'd judge, condemn, abandon me.* Honest? Brave? Are any of us?

No, we tell our stories not as they happened but as we can stand to have them told. If we could really look into other people's minds and hearts at their most hideous and appalling moments, we would surely fear and loathe one another. Yes, I believe the human heart can be that dark. I don't mean humanity isn't capable of great good or beauty but rather that lying alongside those cherubic impulses are diabolical ones. Friendships, marriages, and communities flourish only because we do not know what others *really* think and feel. If we did, no man would ever let a woman look him in the eye. And no woman would want to.

Arguably, none of us even knows the limits of the darkness within our own breast. How many people guilty of crimes of passion or lost in addiction never knew they had it in them till the horrific happened? I sure didn't. No, please don't think anything here is overly honest or laudably brave. If I have said things others are not saying, all that means is we have been silent too long about the gravity of our condition. If we are not crying out with Paul, "Wretched man that I am! Who shall rescue me from this body of death?",[38] we are being neither honest nor brave.

And Yet ...

And yet the most remarkable thing about this miserable reality is that while *we* may not fully know one another or even ourselves, there is One who does. One who pierces through every defense and knows our every motive thoroughly, who knows the evil we fondle and would enact but for the consequences, who knows how we rationalize our small evils on the basis that they aren't the great ones we wish we could do, who knows the dark, the selfish, the wanton, the brutal, the weak, the corrupt, and the malevolent that dwells in us in full Technicolor against which self-deception is our only defense. And surely One who knows all this—this Holy Living God—must loathe us as much as we secretly loathe ourselves.

But here's the thing ...

For reasons I cannot fathom, when this God looks at me, the words that fall from the divine lips are "My beloved son, in whom I'm well pleased."

I shake my head and say, "No, no, you've got me confused with someone else."

The heavens laugh back as though I've made some sort of joke because I've accidently spoken the truth. Yes, someone else *is* in view, but there's been no confusion. I am, in some great mystery, seen both for what I really am and at the same time as if I were someone else—someone greater, better, and holier, someone who has exchanged places with me.

There is a kind of lie we call grace and another we call mercy, and when it comes to such as these, God is the greatest liar of all. When I'm lying on the floor of my living room at 2:00 a.m., broken and hopeless, proclaiming my own unlovability in my rage, envy, and cowardice, this God responds with, *Yes, I already know all that. Now can we please talk of more important things?*

There is, therefore, only one brave and honest way to end this book, and it has nothing to do with me or you or anything we've done or felt. It must end with a declaration of "more important things"—the goodness of God. That is, the God who intends good for us. And further, that the very way God has made the universe is such that one day we shall not miss seeing that goodness.

Yet I hesitate. It may be that your heart is still back in some earlier chapter. If hearing someone say *God is good and desires good for you* smacks of shallow Christian zealotry, that's okay. If my saying this gives you emotional hives, no problem. I only ask you to remember that he who now says it has taken hundreds of pages to get here. Remember what it has cost him to say it. It is no cheap fanaticism but a hard-won conclusion, offered with humility and a recognition that I may not feel as confident about it tomorrow as I do today. I welcome all your challenges, for I realize the inconstancy of my own heart. I vacillate. God knows I vacillate. God does not hate me for vacillating. Today, this hour, I know God is good. Tomorrow you might see it and agree with me, but by then I may have forgotten and will need you to remind me.

But for now, for this hour, I will neither judge nor contradict you. I have stood where you stand and may again. Look down at the spot on the board. What does it say? The square reads, *Cain does not believe God is good.* Of course that's what he believes. Only wait a little …

All that is required of you right now is the smallest possible faith—perhaps the very mustard seed to which Jesus referred. All you need right now is the ability to recognize that your current conclusion, *God is* not *good,* is just as tentative and open to revision as everything else you've ever thought. Faith is not the forcing open of locked doors by main strength. It's merely the continuing belief that doors locked tight today may be found ajar tomorrow. That is all. Belief in a possibility not yet seen, in a future not yet rendered. That's enough for now.

I hope, however, that in these closing pages I may presume to push you an inch further. A belief in an unwritten future may be a first step of faith—and a big one—but I hope we might walk one more square together. If you can agree with me that your future is not yet written, then try this one: Your past is not yet written either.

A More Shocking Truth

In the twilight of this story, I feel compelled to share what is perhaps the single greatest thought I have ever thunk, the single greatest motivation I now possess for pressing forward into life, the most resilient perspective on life I have ever been given. That is either an unworldly large promise or I have an exceedingly low threshold for being impressed. I'll let you decide.

I summon the shade of C. S. Lewis to help me. Listen to the words of George MacDonald as he explains to the dreaming

Lewis the real nature of the journey from the "grey town" to the celestial country in *The Great Divorce*.

> Both good and evil, when they are full grown, become retrospective ... That is what mortals misunderstand. They say of some temporal suffering, "No future bliss can make up for it," not knowing that Heaven, once attained, will work backwards and turn even that agony into a glory. And of some sinful pleasure they say, "Let me have but *this* and I'll take the consequences": little dreaming how damnation will spread back and back into their past and contaminate the pleasure of the sin.
>
> Both processes begin even before death. The good man's past begins to change so that his forgiven sins and remembered sorrows take on the quality of Heaven: the bad man's past already conforms to his badness and is filled with dreariness. And that is why, at the end of all things, when the sun rises here and the twilight turns to blackness down there, the Blessed will say, "We have never lived anywhere except in Heaven," and the Lost, "We were always in Hell." And both will speak truly.[39]

Heaven and hell will work backward to change our past. Oh, my head! Can it be?

Can Lewis be right that we will one day look at *everything* we've done here through the eyes of either heaven or hell? That our final destination will somehow recolor, revise, reinterpret all our best and worst moments so that we will actually see them as having participated in a foretaste of heaven or hell?

If so, then the implication is staggering. It means that *only* in that day will the final meaning of each square on the board be established. It means that even some squares that contained snakes may turn out to have been the pathways to gardens, while some containing ladders will reveal themselves to have led only to trap doors and musty attics.

If so, then whether we know it or not, whether we like it or not, whether we intend it or not, this *is* the nature of the journey we're actually on. This is the game all the various squares of the board make up. It's all about the answer to the great and final question—What will the events of our lives mean?

I've slowly come to understand that Lewis is not attempting an act of theological trickery or rhetoric. He is merely recognizing one of the facts of being a temporal creature. To be a creature is to swim in the liquidity of change. God alone is eternal and unchanging. God alone sees things *as they are*. We see things only *as they mean* ... and meanings change. They change all the time. They will not assume their final character till a greater morning dawns.

> We see things only as they mean ... and meanings change.

But this is not merely a future reality. We see it at work already, happening in real time. Present realities are changing settled past events, even now. Don't believe me? Try to watch an episode of *The Cosby Show*.

How Shall We Then Live: The Final Invitation

The principle of the changeable past may be the most important ever articulated for persons like you and me—people who stagger limping through life with self-inflicted wounds and self-made sorrows, people who can't lay down their afflictions because their afflictions are in some real sense merited. This is the divine answer to Cain's ceaseless bellowing as he wanders through the world marked for all to see. I wish I could say to him, "Oh, Cain, you resent the mark you bear. But it doesn't *mean* what you think it does ... or at least it need not mean that forever."

I wish he could believe me. I wish you could. The past *is* changeable. It's changing right now under your hand. What we do from here out will define and redefine the meaning of that past horror. The point is worth restating a final time, now with new gravity: That awful life-destroying choice you made is not half so defining as the choices you will now make. You are now on precisely the journey that will determine whether your horrible choice was prescient of heaven or a harbinger of hell. Yes, you have that much power over your past.

Don't misunderstand. I am not telling you to work harder, have a positive attitude, or pull yourself up and restore your own life. I'm not such a hypocrite. Your bootstraps will not bear the weight of all that tugging. The truth is you may have many more hellacious things ahead of you. Your life may get more prosperous or it may tank. I can't know any of that. My point is that none of that really matters. Yes, I know it matters insofar as none of us want to suffer, but it doesn't ultimately matter in the sense that the hope necessary for making life livable isn't held hostage to circumstance. Joy will not always be a victim of the dark passenger. Heaven is capable of working its way back into your story, into the square you're standing on now … if you will let it.

Murdering his brother was not the most defining choice Cain made. That we are not witnesses to the rest of his life doesn't change anything. In fact, it may be the point. It's true of us all. The greatest changes in the soul are often not visible from without. They remain unrecorded even by the inspired biographer. But make no mistake, Cain took a journey just like us. A journey from his failure to … where? His options were the same as ours.

Cain may have embraced his rage against God, against his parents, against his dead brother and maintained the "unfairness" of his punishment. If he did, that mistake would grow to be at least as great as the one that destroyed him in the first place. What hell does with such recalcitrance is not to be imagined.

But perhaps he did not make this second mistake. Perhaps a day came when he began to see both the gravity of his sin and the generosity of his God. Perhaps he eventually discovered grace enough to see something more than failure in the mark he bore—the odious blemish that identified him to his brethren as a murderer.

The mark that made him an outcast.

The mark that symbolized his self-inflicted suffering.

Perhaps, just perhaps, as the long weary years of his life wore on, he began to suspect that this mark, without ceasing to be any of those ghastly things, was also the means by which God spoke the words "My beloved son"—the mark that was his protection, nay, his very salvation. In a great and heavenly reversal of meaning, perhaps that hideous mark became for him an invitation to meet the God of the perpetual present and, in that meeting, find redemption.

Perhaps to us, his children, the same opportunity is now offered.

SURVIVING
THE LEGAL SYSTEM

Two prison inmates were telling each other their stories. The first was serving two years for a violent assault on his wife and child. The second was serving fifteen years for having two grams of cocaine in his pocket instead of just one.

The second man was now angry, pacing the cell, complaining bitterly about the unfairness of the legal system.

"You're absolutely right," said the first. "The only thing worse than the criminal justice system is not having one."

THIS IS A PRACTICAL APPENDIX WITH LITTLE OF DEVOTIONAL value in it. If criminality hasn't been part of your story, you probably don't need to read it. If, however, a criminal charge is on the menu, then here are a number of things I wish I'd known beforehand on surviving the justice system. Obviously, none of this should be considered legal advice. This is only my experience.

I still get a random case of shivers occasionally over all the ways my situation could have been worse. I hesitate to credit to divine providence what *didn't* happen because I don't want to drag God into my crappy choices as if God has nothing better to do than prevent our bad choices from being worse. It's not that

I don't think God does this, but only that I can't know how such things work. Divine mercy and human idiocy are often related like different sides of the same coin.

For example, Lorelai had sent her children off to her mother's house for the evening. I later learned from my lawyer that, had they been in the house—merely *in* the house—the whole thing would have gone much worse for me, both in sentencing and in the media. People rightly get weird when kids are involved.

Another irony I'll call it for lack of something better: Unbeknownst to me, a member of my own congregation worked in the criminal justice system and happened to be sitting at some monitor somewhere reviewing the daily arrest records at the moment I was booked. My name came across her screen, and in what must have been the most surreal moment of her day, she had the presence of mind to immediately call Denise to find out what was going on. Dear Cathy proceeded to walk with us through the whole journey, recommending a defense attorney she trusted, coming to nearly every court appearance, and explaining all the things we couldn't have known about the system.

Beyond all others, she offered the sagest perspective: "No one ever said the criminal justice system is just, it just *is*." Without her, we would have been awash in paralysis. Her efforts to mitigate the needless pain of our cluelessness prompted me to write this pragmatic appendix.

The System

The first thing you should know is that the criminal justice system is overbuilt. It has to be. It deals with many people who are habitually screwed up. The hardest of hard cases pass through its halls. This means it's not really constructed to deal with someone like you who, I hope, are not a repeat, habitual offender. (If you are, God bless you, hang in there; I just don't have much experiential wisdom to give you.) If you're like me, you're a person who screwed up without meaning to hurt anyone. You've done wrong, for sure, but you have no intention of ever darkening the doors of a courtroom again. That will make little difference to how the system perceives you. In all likelihood you will be treated like one of the harder cases—because in a holding cell and in a courtroom, we all look the same to police, prosecutors, and juries.

Second, you should know that once the criminal justice system is involved, all possibilities of reconciliatory interaction with your accuser-victim go out the window. The system is constructed from the ground up to keep accuser and accused apart. This is actually one of those realities that flow out of the last point. The default assumption of those who run the justice system *has to be* that you are a potentially violent flight risk bent on doing something worse if given a chance. I hope you can at least understand that they *have* to think this way because they're actually used to dealing with those kinds of people, and again, we all look alike to them.

So this means they will put a "no contact order" in place. You will not, as a term of your bond, be permitted to interact with the complainant. In general, this is understandable and wise, but it will make a mockery of any attempt to do justice by negotiation. You should not contact, try to explain, beg for mercy, or in any way attempt to talk your accusers out of exercising their legal rights. Nor should you have someone else—a family member, pastor, mutual friend—do it for you. That will all be used against you by viciously creative prosecutors.

It really puts Jesus's words about leaving your sacrifice at the altar and going to make peace with your accuser in a different light.[40] If any party wishes to mediate a resolution between you and the person you hurt, it must happen before the cops are involved. Once they are, you must let that idea go and start thinking about your defense.

Police. As I said, if you're interacting with law enforcement for the first and only time, prepare yourself to be treated like a habitual offender. It will be your job—your counsel's job—to persuade them otherwise. But till that happens, just fasten your seat belt and prepare for some indignities.

As I sat in the final holding tank before bail came through, I listened to the young men in there go back and forth about how they just wished the cops would process them and get them upstairs before they "missed the hot meal." One groused about how unfair this all was because he was due to appear in court in another county that day but couldn't because he was under arrest for whatever he'd done here in Kent County. He then got into a yelling match with the cop over something, insults were traded, and when the cop came to "take them upstairs," he took everybody but this guy in order to "teach him his place."

When Denise got the call about bail, the officer encouraged her to leave me in overnight to "let him think about what he's done." See the logic? Since the only way you end up in the pokey is that some cop arrested you, every other cop in the place assumes you're guilty, and sadly statistics say they're probably right. It's ugly and dehumanizing but entirely predictable.

I don't know how it could be different, but you can't afford to believe the police are interested in your welfare. The nice detective who initially took my report recorded that interaction, but I didn't know that till I was done telling my story. He even asked, "So does there happen to be any video or anything like that? If so, it won't make your situation worse, but we do need to recover it." Of course there wasn't any such video, but later my attorney laughed and said far from not making my situation worse, had there been, new charges would have applied, and I most certainly would have gone to prison for a long time. Do not mistake rapport for sympathy—the police are trained to get answers from you. They are generally good people doing a hard job, but they are not looking out for your interests. If the police are at your door and you didn't call them, assume they are "protecting and serving" someone else at the moment.

Prosecutors. Prosecutors have one job: to get the strongest conviction they believe they can prove. Chief prosecutors are often elected officials and do not want to be seen as soft on crime. The initial charge that comes down may have very little to do with what you actually did. It may only be the bar from which negotiations begin. However, as was my case, if the complainants resist reduction, prosecutors will often not budge, particularly once the media has shown interest in the case. They don't want to be perceived as being soft on victims' rights either.

So in my case, the charge to which I pled isn't actually what I did. Oh, I looked in the window (I admit that) but the "surveilling" charge, as my lawyer explained it to me, was a fairly recent stiffening of old misdemeanor peeping meant to update the code to the digital era. It was intended for when there *was* video or something similar. Since my case didn't involve that, a point the prosecutor conceded, my attorney thought he was testing the limits of the new law. All these vagaries, he told me, meant that if I lost the first round, my case had good appellate possibilities and could even go to the Michigan Supreme Court if I wanted.

I didn't want.

I didn't have $50,000 to throw at this, nor did I want to put my family through three more years of hell. Plus the system is set up so that if you take your day in court and lose, you face minimum sentencing, which in my case was two to four years in prison. The goal is to keep people who are clearly guilty from glutting the courts with needless trials hoping to get off on a technicality. But it also means if you choose to exercise your constitutional rights, they make you pay for it. "It isn't just, it just *is.*"

What's one to do? I'll tell you. If you're me, you take a plea for a crime you didn't commit as a substitute for the crime you did commit and hope the judge is a decent enough human being to see through all the crap.

Thankfully, he was. So I have little to complain about.

Judges. Judges are often elected. They are politicians. Remember that. Lady Justice may be blindfolded, but she also needs votes. As such, the court is a place where optics matter. And since the judge is god in that room, anything you say or do that puts the judge in an awkward position will go badly for you. Do not argue, disagree, or correct the judge. You have a lawyer for that. Remember, the court wants nothing from you but contrition. Anything else can and will be used against you.

Your Counsel. You need an attorney. Full stop. I met a pastor who, a few years before my debacle, had been convicted of indecent exposure based on a phone photo. He didn't think he needed an attorney, because being plainly guilty, he was just going to own it and take his medicine. He went to prison for a very long time.

Without an expert in your corner, the system will roll right over you. Not because anyone does anything malicious but because the system is adversarial by design. It's built to work by means of opposing pressures. The prosecution pushes one way as hard as it can, the defense pushes the opposite direction with equal strength, and the judge in the middle moderates and makes sure everyone plays by the rules. If you don't have counsel, you'll get steamrolled by a system that just doesn't function without that counter pressure.

You should also know that your lawyer's job is not to make the guilty go free but to provide that counter pressure on your behalf. Note: I'm speaking here as a citizen who wants the republic to survive. There are bad lawyers out there who do make it their mission to help guilty people go free. We all hate them. We hate what they do when we see the effects of it on the evening news. Judges don't like them either. If you want one of them, roll your dice.

I had an ethical lawyer. While he was explaining to us in his office all the horrible things that were about to happen, I lost my head at one moment and shouted, "Well, what do we have to do to beat this thing?" not knowing even exactly what that phrase meant. He looked at me sadly and said, "We'd have to prove you didn't look in the window. Did you look in the window?" I nodded and deflated. Honest lawyers suck as much as other kinds, just for different reasons.

As I watched this all play out, however, I did discover a number of things about lawyers I wish I had known beforehand.

Pit Bulls v. Great Danes. As I suggested above, I think there are two sorts of defense attorneys. I was a little put out initially that my lawyer wasn't screaming and yelling about the injustice done to me—you know, trying to get the guilty guy off on a technicality. I thought that's what defense attorneys were supposed to do—be pit bulls. Lie, cheat, steal, do whatever is necessary to get you off. This perspective, I assume, is the product of watching too much television.

My lawyer never said anything even remotely untrue. He was calm and forthright. He conceded facts to the prosecutor. A real gentleman. All in all he was more like a Great Dane than a pit bull.

But when push came to shove, the very day we had to either take the plea or go to trial, he disappeared into the judge's chambers for a half hour, and when he came out, he said, "Congratulations, you're not going to jail," meaning *that* particular sentence was off the table in the plea deal. I asked him what he'd said. He replied, "I told the judge your moral compass had bent under a great deal of pressure but had not broken, but incarceration might break it for good." I shudder to this day at what all that might have meant, but it produced an epiphany. This lawyer had spent his entire career being completely frank with judges. They knew he would not snow them or bluster just to get his client off. They knew he was a Great Dane. So when he said my case did not warrant incarceration, the judge believed him.

If I'd had a pit bull, I would have gone to trial, lost, and been sent to jail. My Great Dane may not have aggressively raged against the system on my behalf, but because the system knew he was not a showman, I got the benefit of his thirty years of hard-won credibility.

Some lawyers speak softly. Some carry big sticks. Choose your counsel carefully.

When to ignore them. One of the first things my lawyer did was gag me. No public conversations, no public admissions, no discussing things with anyone outside my family. This is a boilerplate technique of a defense attorney, designed to keep you from making your situation worse. For me, however, it somewhat backfired, and in hindsight I believe I should have ignored this advice in one situation.

The elders and the whole church were waiting for a public apology from me, which I was equally desirous of giving … which my attorney would not allow me to give. It took nearly eight months for the legal stuff to wind down. Eight months of silence imposed by my lawyer, which, since the elders didn't involve themselves in the legal aspects of my situation, they could only assume was ongoing impenitence.

So something to know: You should always follow your lawyer's advice … except when you shouldn't.

Understand: Your lawyer has only one responsibility—*to limit your legal liability.* To accomplish that, they will sacrifice everything else. That is their job. Respect it.

By analogy, it's like your CPA's only job is to file your taxes properly. She can't tell you whether a Disney vacation will be good for your family or whether a weekend in the Poconos is good for your marriage. If she tells you to go, it will be because there's a tax advantage, and if she tells you not to, it's because of some tax liability. Don't blame her if her advice costs you your marriage. Your marriage was *yours* to protect, not hers. She's only a subject-matter expert you hire for that subject. It's not her responsibility to help you achieve your "best life now."

Same with a trial lawyer. You're paying him to limit your legal liability, and in doing so, he may cost you your marriage or family. That is not his fault. It's what you've paid him to do.

I know a man who, in the middle of his divorce, had allegations of abuse made against him by his young kids (with a little help from his nearly-ex-wife). The accusations were ultimately shown to be without merit, but for several months he lived in moment-to-moment fear of being arrested. He sought legal counsel from a criminal defense attorney, and the advice given was "Give up parental rights. If they've been coached into saying these things once, it'll happen again. Leave your kids now or eventually go to jail." *That* is how a defense attorney thinks—limit your legal liability even if it means abandoning your children. It's your lawyer's job to say things like this. It's then up to you to make a choice based on *your* values.

In my case, the silence my lawyer enjoined, which I obeyed, doomed nearly every relationship in that church. The congregants' only sources of information were the elders and the newspapers. The former believed me impenitent, and the latter thought me a pervert. When the court case finally wound down and I made my public confession to the church, it was met with stony silence.

You have more assets that need protecting than just your legal liability. Don't make the mistake of thinking an expert in the law is qualified to guard them all.

The Media. If the media has taken an interest in you, I'm sorry. To this day, they remain the people I find it most difficult to forgive. Ninety percent of the long-term harm to me and my family is rooted in their insatiable need to turn a tragic story of depression and obsession into a sensationalized sex-crazed rampage.

It is a fault in me—I concede it—but I still smolder over how easily they twisted my story into something sexy and salable and then dropped it. I have never had a reporter come back to me and see how my life turned out. No follow up. No "rest of the story." And forgiveness is rendered all the harder because I have no name or face to go with it. It is rage expressed at an impersonal agency. Useless rage.

So don't expect them to get it right. It's not personal. Whether you make the news depends entirely on what else happens in the community that day. God forgive me, but that night I actually prayed, *Dear Lord, let there be a sexier tragedy somewhere in West Michigan tonight.* Nope, here came the news vans down my driveway.

My only advice for you is to just hide. Let it pass. The media will lose interest in you quickly enough. Just don't google yourself, and for all that's high and holy, don't read the comments following the news stories and social media posts. Just. Don't.

Plea Deals. Finally, a couple of thoughts on the conclusion of the legal stuff. Since your case is unique, I can't tell you whether to take your day in court or take a plea. In my bitterest moment, I wanted to go to trial, not caring how long they put me away for, just so my lawyer would have the chance to put Lorelai on the stand and make her confess her part in what happened. Show the texts. Show the list of names I had of other men she'd done this to. Prove to the whole world that, yes, I was a perpetrator, but I'd also been used. I wanted it so badly.

Thank God for Cathy, my friend on the inside of the system. She reminded me that the real point was Denise and the kids. They still needed me, and by some mystery I couldn't fathom, they still wanted me.

So I made a deal with God: If I took this plea so my family could get on with life, someday I'd write the book that laid it all bare and made Lorelai accept her share in the shame. I bellowed, like a fevered Scarlett O'Hara, "If I have to lie, steal, cheat or kill, as God is my witness, I'll never be hungry again!" I'm ashamed to admit it, but it's the truth. I thought like this, and perhaps you know the feeling. It's the square I was on for a long time.

It just goes to show you how gently and patiently God moves the human soul. Here I am, years later, on a very different square, writing this book, and I have no desire to shame, call out, or indict. You may say I've done so passive-aggressively at moments. You may be right. All I can say is that my emotions have not risen up in acrimonious rebellion in the writing of it. This final section came out of my keyboard with the same disinterest as anything else in the book. I believe myself to be merely reporting it as part of the journey without prejudice to her. You may choose to believe me or not. You've been making that choice since the beginning of the book.

The final point is this: Most people don't write books about their adventures as I am doing, so you need to be aware that taking a plea may end your capacity to tell your story. Taking a plea deal is an admission of guilt, and you're required to say as much in front of the judge. I can't tell you whether it's better in your case to have it over with and be silenced or to prolong the agony for the sake of making your side known. I can only hope to encourage you by saying that, for as grave as this choice feels, the more important choices lie within you. The sort of person you will be when you emerge from the other end of the legal stuff is being shaped now. So sit still. Be silent. Listen. Can you hear God in it yet?

ENDNOTES

1. 1 John 3:12.
2. Sir Walter Scott, "Marmion" (Edinburgh: Archibald Constable and Company, 1808), canto 17.
3. C. S. Lewis, Miracles (London: Geoffrey Bles, 1947), 73.
4. Matthew 18:8 ESV.
5. Philippians 4:10–13.
6. Reference to "10,000 Reasons (Bless the Lord)," 2011 Shout! Publishing, sixsteps Music, Said and Done Music and Thankyou Music (PRS), admin. in the United States and Canada at EMICMGPUBLISHING.com, sixsteps Music and Said and Done Music admin. at EMICMGPUBLISHING.com, Thankyou Music admin. Worldwide.
7. 1 Kings 21:4 ESV.
8. C. S. Lewis, "Meditations on a Toolshed," in *God in the Dock: Essays on Theology and Ethics*, ed. Walter Hooper (Grand Rapids, MI: Eerdmans Publishing, 1970), 213.
9. Jerry Sittser, *A Grace Disguised* (Grand Rapids, MI: Zondervan, 2004), 61.
10. Mother Teresa and Brain Kolodiejchuk, *Mother Teresa: Come Be My Light: The Private Writings of the Saint of Calcutta* (Image Doubleday, 2009).
11. Sittser, *A Grace Disguised*, 45–46.
12. Isaiah 45:15 ESV.
13. Psalm 88:18 NIV.
14. C. S. Lewis, *The Magician's Nephew* (London: The Bodley Head, 1955), 102.
15. David Mamet, *Theatre* (New York: Farrar, Straus and Giroux, 2010).

16. Matthew 7:1–2 ESV.

17. 1 Timothy 4:2.

18. 1 Corinthians 10–13.

19. C. S. Lewis, *The Great Divorce* (London: Geoffrey Bles, 1946), 57.

20. Reference to "Find Us Faithful," 1987 Jonathan Mark Music (Admin. Gaither Copyright Management) and Birdwing Music (Admin. EMI Christian Music Publishing), recorded by Steve Green, 1988.

21. For those of you who are into such things, survey the εὐδοκέω and ἀρέσκω domains in Greek and the חָפֵץ and רָצָה domains in Hebrew.

22. The Hebrew here is less clear to me, but in Greek consider the δοκιμάζω and to a lesser extent the κρίνω domains.

23. Philippians 3:13–14 NIV.

24. 2 Timothy 2:15 NIV.

25. Romans 8:38–39.

26. Matthew 16:16 ESV.

27. Luke 4:38–29.

28. John 21:17 ESV.

29. Galatians 2:11-13.

30. Acts 13:5 and 15:36–41 preserve the record of John Mark's failure, while Philemon 24 and 2 Timothy 2:11 imply his restoration—a restoration so thorough that he is even traditionally credited as the author of the Gospel of Mark.

31. Isaiah 64:6.

32. C. S. Lewis, *The Voyage of the Dawn Treader* (London: Geoffrey Bles, 1952), 102.

33. 1 John 3:20.

34. Romans 5:8 NIV.

35. J. K. Rowling, *Harry Potter and the Goblet of Fire* (New York, NY: Scholastic, 2002).

36. Mark 1:15; Matthew 6:12, 14–15.

37. Reference to "Find Us Faithful," 1987 Jonathan Mark Music (Admin. Gaither Copyright Management) and Birdwing Music (Admin. EMI Christian Music Publishing), recorded by Steve Green, 1988.

38. Romans 7:24.

39. Lewis, *The Great Divorce*, 62.

40. Matthew 5:23–26.

If you found *The Bellowing of Cain* helpful,
please consider posting a review on a retail website
or your social media. We would appreciate your help
in spreading the word about this important book.

For additional resources, to interact with the author,
or for links to the ebook or audiobook editions,
please visit the website:

www.bellowingofcain.com

To order additional copies for your ministry,
staff, students, or friends, you may
contact Iron Stream Media directly:

orders@ironstreammedia.com

888-811-9934